# BLACK MAFIA QUEEN

# BLACK MAFIA QUEEN

## Dr. TONESA WELCH
### with H. COREY MILLS

**Foreword by
Vivica A. Fox**

KENSINGTON PUBLISHING CORP.
kensingtonbooks.com

DAFINA BOOKS are published by

Kensington Publishing Corp.
900 Third Avenue
New York, NY 10022

All Kensington Titles, Imprints, and Distributed Lines are available at special quantity discounts for bulk purchases for sales promotions, premiums, fundraising, and educational or institutional use. Special book excerpts or customized printings can also be created to fit specific needs. For details, write or phone the office of the Kensington Special Sales Manager: Kensington Publishing Corp., 900 Third Avenue, New York, NY 10022, Attn: Special Sales Department, Phone: 1-800-221-2647.

Library of Congress Control Number: On file

The DAFINA logo is a trademark of Kensington Publishing Corp.

ISBN: 978-1-4967-5276-5
First Kensington Hardcover Edition: March 2026

ISBN: 978-1-4967-5278-9 (ebook)

10 9 8 7 6 5 4 3 2 1

Printed in the United States of America

The authorized representative in the EU for product safety and compliance
is eucomply OU, Parnu mnt 139b-14, Apt 123
Tallinn, Berlin 11317, hello@eucompliancepartner.com

*To my granddaughters*

When I first came home from prison, everyone told me to write a book. At first, in 2012, coming straight out of prison, I felt it was not clear why or what I had to contribute to the world. The thoughts in my head were: What had I done? What did I have to share? What more was there to talk about besides my rise and fall? What was I proud of?

I had a lot of work to do understand about me and my life. I was afraid. I didn't know if I was at the beginning of my life or the end. I prayed this life I returned to couldn't be it. I knew and trusted my God that He wasn't finished with me yet. I held on to hope for the future and the next generation; and when I authored a book, I wanted to give people, especially my beautiful granddaughters, something more.

I wanted you all to feel proud of me, not only knowing me as Tonesa Welch, First Lady of BMF, a drug queen, but as an extraordinary woman who was never too strong or vulnerable to look within—no matter how ugly the scars—and accept the flaws that became my strength.

To see me as someone who not only accepted change, but also took accountability and responsibility for her own actions. Someone you all could hold your heads up high for and be proud to say where you come from.

And to understand I didn't feel so good about who I once was—and to understand why I committed some of the mistakes I made along the way—but to be encouraged to never let the past dictate the promises of tomorrow.

# Contents

# CONTENTS

# Foreword

As a woman, I find that Tonesa Welch's journey as the Queen-pin of the Black Mafia Family resonates deeply with me. Her story transcends mere power and influence; it embodies the spirit of breaking barriers, defying expectations, and navigating a world dominated by men. Through her strength, intelligence, and unwavering determination, Tonesa carved out her own path, leaving an indelible mark on history.

In addition to her remarkable rise as the queenpin, Tonesa Welch's legacy is enriched by her role as a devoted mother to three sons, exemplifying the strength and resilience of a woman who defied norms in a male-dominated domain. Tonesa's ascent to prominence was marked by trials and tribulations. Beyond her role as the queenpin, she also held the title of the First Lady of the Black Mafia Family, underscoring her integral role in the organization's success. Yet, beneath the veneer of power, there lay a woman who endured unimaginable hardships.

Throughout her journey, Tonesa confronted the stark reality of domestic abuse, a silent struggle often overshadowed by her public persona. Behind closed doors, she bore the scars of physical and emotional trauma, fighting to maintain her dignity and self-worth in the face of adversity. Her trials extended beyond abuse, encompassing the heartache of losing loved ones, casualties of a perilous lifestyle. Each loss reinforced the sacrifices demanded by her path, propelling her to push harder and reach further in her pursuit of success.

Yet, the ultimate test of Tonesa's resilience came with her incarceration, a fate threatening to shatter her dreams. Stripped of freedom and separated from all she held dear, she faced the daunting task of rebuilding her life anew. But true to form, Tonesa refused to be defined by her circumstances. Behind bars, she found solace in words, using her time to reflect, grow, and chart a new course. With unwavering determination, she emerged from confinement, stronger and wiser. In the aftermath of her release, Tonesa confronted the challenge of reinvention, and, with characteristic resilience and unwavering belief in herself, embraced the opportunity for growth and transformation.

Today, Tonesa Welch stands as a beacon of hope and inspiration, a testament to perseverance, resilience, and unwavering determination. Her story serves as a reminder that no obstacle is insurmountable—no setback too great to overcome. Join me as we embark on a journey through the extraordinary life of a woman who dared to defy the odds and emerged victorious in the face of adversity.

*—Vivica A. Fox, American actress, film producer, director, and TV host*

# Tonesa's Introduction

## Stripped of All, Yet Rising Above

The high that my cocaine empire sold our customers only lasted twenty minutes . . . but the euphoria from the Birkin bags their money bought me lingered as long as that soft leather was hanging on my shoulder.

I grew up middle-class in Detroit. My parents worked for the Ford Motor Company, and I thought that's where I would work, too. I surely wasn't the kind of girl you'd think would play an instrumental role in helping to start the largest Black cocaine-distribution empire in America, which came to be known as the infamous Black Mafia Family.

Why and how, then, did a nice middle-class girl like me become one of the top cocaine-distribution mafia queens in America? It wasn't because of the drugs, I can tell you that. I dealt with addiction early on in my drug-dealing career, and by the time our operation went big-time, orchestrating five-hundred-kilo shipments from the major Mexican cartels, and distributing thousands of kilos nationally for tens of millions of dollars, I had gotten clean. I would, however, take the money I earned from people getting high off our blow . . . and blow it on an entirely different addiction.

With the same beautiful green paper that my customers rolled up to snort our product, I'd go on $20,000-plus shopping sprees on Rodeo Drive at least once a week—and I always paid in cash. In my mansion, I had a closet the size of many people's apartments, filled top-to-bottom with designer clothes. I even put a couch in there so my girlfriends could drink champagne while I showed off my latest purchases.

Why did I care about fashion to such an insane degree? Well, it was rather simple.

The answer is, I felt the same desire that motivated so many other women: I wanted to feel pretty.

The only difference between me and most other women was that I generated millions of dollars to pursue and fulfill this desire to the $n$th degree. The way I gained those millions was unusual, wildly destructive to others, and very illegal.

Now this brings up another question. Why was I so obsessed with my looks? My half brothers, from a different father, were Black, but they had fair skin and green eyes. I was darker skinned, with brown eyes, so in the eyes of my stepfather, who raised me (and who was also darker skinned), that made me *lesser* than my brothers. Like so many women of color, I had severe low-esteem issues because of my looks.

Believe me when I say, you tend to feel really pretty on Rodeo Drive with $50,000 in cash and a Black Card you're not afraid to use. It's hard to have low self-esteem when you're trying on $5,000 dresses at Gucci, Louis Vuitton, and Yves Saint Laurent stores. I never left the house with less than $20,000 in clothing on my skin; that certainly made me feel less bad about being darker than my half brothers.

When the law finally caught up to me, and the Feds raided my mansion, the first thing they did was take pictures of my closet. For some weird reason, the female prosecutor was obsessed with my closet, and she kept bringing it up in court hearings, to the point that the male judge had to tell her to shut up about it. In retrospect, I wonder if her obsession stemmed from envy.

A few years later, I was trying on a very different kind of fashion: a puke-green prison smock courtesy of the Federal Prison

# TONESA'S INTRODUCTION

Camp at Victorville, California, where I began my fifty-seven-month sentence on federal money-laundering charges. Prison stripped away any and every crutch I used to prop up my self-esteem externally, and it left me facing the one thing I had been unwilling to face my entire life: me, myself, and I.

My new home prompted me to ask myself some really loaded questions. Who was I without five-figure shopping sprees, six-figure cars, seven-figure mansions, private jets, and a seat managing an eight-figure-per-year drug empire? Well, as it turns out, I had lots of time to find that out as I swept and mopped the floor of the prison chapel, day in and day out. It was my assigned job at the camp. Can you believe it? It was just me, my mop, and God.

When they stripped me of my designer clothing at the intake, they also took away every external crutch I had been using to cover up the deeply rooted issues I hadn't dealt with in my life. For the first time in my existence, I had to face my spiritually naked self. By the time I had made it into the women's federal prison therapy programs in Dublin, California, I was experiencing something I'd never encountered before: other women in my program, as well as the counselors, loving me as a human being, without any external validation of my status. They truly loved me just for who I am as a human being.

For the first time in my life, I experienced relating to fellow human beings, and they relating to me, based on the content of my character rather than the quality of my clothes or how much money and credit cards I had stuffed in my wallet. In prison, behind bars, we were equals, whether we were considered to be pretty or not by society's standards. All of us were equal in our aspirations to get our lives on the right track, right our wrongs, and become good role models rather than destructive forces in our communities.

Once I got out, I devoted myself to supporting other families with incarcerated family members in order to get through the ups and downs of the prison journey that I went through.

# TONESA'S INTRODUCTION

This is where I have ended up in my journey. But it didn't begin this way. It started with one of the craziest stories of money, drugs, hunger for power, and lust for beauty you've ever heard . . . And here's a unique twist . . .

This book is written in collaboration with my son, Corey Mills. Corey lived through large parts of this story, and—as a professional writer—he is helping me tell it. Though most of the narrative is my own story, there will also be several chapters that tell the story through his eyes, as my son, while all of this was going down.

—*Dr. Tonesa Welch, First Lady of the Black Mafia Family*

# Corey's Introduction

## Picking Up Bad Habits

Get this, I came into this world on August 11, 1989, which is the same day and month as when my mother was born. Two weeks late, I arrived just in time before the doctors had to force me out. The last of three sons, I'm certainly a momma's boy and have shared quite a close relationship with my birthday twin since the day I was born. *What do you give the man, woman, or child who has everything?* A lesson.

Growing up with parents who hustled and made an insane amount of money came with its privileges and drawbacks, like any other household, I would imagine. Living life in such a way un-doubtedly came with some hardships along the way, but it also taught a valuable lesson or two throughout the journey.

Many have this preconceived idea of what it looks like to grow up with parents who sold drugs; but to tell the truth, it all seemed quite ordinary to me. Honestly, my mom seems to have kept me sheltered. There weren't mountains of blow on the kitchen table, addicts coming in and out of the house, or a lot of physical abuse in the home.

At a young age, it appeared to me that we were comfortably middle-class and quickly climbed the above-the-average income of any street hustler and even many Wall Street CEOs. To a cer-tain degree, I grew up bearing the weight of the family business in school and in my personal life. I felt my parents' secret was my secret—and that it was necessary to keep most of my friends at arm's length. In my opinion, having a life shrouded in secrecy held me back, and it was a hindrance to my development as a young man, but you couldn't have told me that then.

"What will I do now?" I whispered to my brother as we sat on the couch while the DEA, FBI, and IRS ransacked our house. I watched as agents confiscated my laptop and modem of my computer for investigation purposes. It was my connection to the world, to friends, and the closeted space I invited a select few in my school or outside the family to get to know who I truly was or how extravagant my life was.

Jason stayed quiet as one of the SWAT men chimed in, "You won't be able to get all the shoes and stuff you want now."

*What?*

I hadn't thought about how my life would be affected financially or materially. Not to sound cocky, but I had everything. At the age of sixteen, I already had a brand-new Range Rover, an iced-out Jacob watch, shoes and clothes galore from all the best designers—Gucci, Prada, Lacoste. You name it, I owned it. Quite frankly, I never had struggled in my entire life or had seen my mother penniless; it was absolutely a foreign concept. Be that as it may, I was referring to the fact I would be cut off from the new burgeoning social media, like MySpace and Facebook.

"What is going on?" my grandmother Carol asked him.

"Your daughter and her husband are in a lot of trouble," the SWAT guy remarked.

"Husband?" She shook her head, with her hands between her thighs. It was cold and still very early in the morning when the house was descended on by federal agents; we were all still clueless as to what was actually happening. Terry, my stepfather, had been arrested before, and he was quickly released the next day, so it didn't actually dawn on me that this was not the same situation. This was the end of the hurrah. I guess the agent was right. My days of buying every shoe, or whatever else I wanted, were over, but I only scowled at him without uttering another word.

# COREY'S INTRODUCTION

*Let him believe whatever he wants,* I told myself.

"She isn't married," my grandmother responded back.

"Hmm, well, be that as it may. We're just following orders."

My grandmother shut up and proceeded to remain quiet.

I watched as they came back and forth from the bottom floors of our home that descended from a hill, instead of upward like most homes.

Separated from us, my mother was in the kitchen, where law enforcement asked her a series of questions, trying to break her.

Suddenly an agent, coming from my closet, brought my safe with him. I held the key on me, and because I was a minor, they weren't allowed to search me. They subsequently pulled me into the kitchen.

"What's in the safe?" a female agent asked my mother.

"I don't know. Just kid stuff, it's his."

The woman and several other agents looked over at me for confirmation.

"Just some money from my vending machine and change really," I added.

"Okay, okay."

They appeared satisfied with my response and moved on. I was nervous as hell not exactly knowing if I answered the question to my mom's expectations, but she seemed reassured with my response. They all did. She hadn't lied to them. She honestly had no idea what I stored in the heavy Saflok, which I tucked away behind my jeans and jackets in my walk-in closet.

Still, it wasn't quite the truth. As a result, from my affinity for cars and Terry's love of automobiles as well, he would give me a spare key to every automobile we owned. This included a Maybach 62, Aston Martin, two Bentley Continental GTs, and several Range Rovers. Several documents confirming the authenticity of some of the diamonds he owned were also tucked away in the safe.

# COREY'S INTRODUCTION

In what felt like an eternity as we waited for it to be over, the agents still searched, coming up with nothing. No money, no drugs, and no weapons anywhere could be found. I still felt uneasy. What if they decided to open up the safe, after all? I had just lied to federal agents. I thought, *What harm could I cause myself or my mom?* If they thought she coached me to give that answer, could she be slapped with some type of charge?

The moment I had heard my mom yelling, "Corey, Jay . . . it's the police," I had rushed out of bed, wearing nothing but my boxers. I questioned if I should make a run for it through the door in my room. My bedroom had direct access to the backyard, and if I went then, I could have possibly made it out and away from the raid.

Instead, I froze, unable to decide what to do, just before the agents had barged in with semiautomatic rifles drawn toward me.

*"Freeze!"*

I had put my hands in the air, and they escorted me away to join my brother and grandmother, who were in the living room on the first floor of our home. *Damn,* I could have gotten away.

Another agent flew into the kitchen, with a determined look on his face. "We're going to need to get into that safe. Who has the key?"

"I do!" I said as I looked in my mother's direction for reassurance.

"Okay," she responded. "Give them the key."

While my mother directed me to go fetch the key, the agent put his arm out, signaling for me to hold on. "Just tell us where it is!"

"In the drawer, on top of my dresser," I replied.

He shot out of the kitchen before returning a short while later with the keys in his hand. Lo and behold, a treasure trove of car keys and other sensitive documents lay right in front of them.

# COREY'S INTRODUCTION

Astonished, they had almost looked past it. My little white lie seemed sincere enough for them to believe until what must have been a higher-up gave the order to search through my belongings, anyway.

Agitated, the female agent shot me a domineering look. "I thought you said there wasn't anything in here?"

I had almost gotten over on her, but the severity of the offense weighed heavily on my mom. I essentially was too young to have made that decision in their eyes.

"You said it was just kid stuff in here. This looks like car keys."

"I . . . I thought it was!" Stammering, my mother's look of sheer shock was convincing enough for them to not hound her about it—at least, not while I was present.

How did I know to lie? Who taught me to think so quickly on my feet?

Little did they know that from a very early age, picking up bad habits was something I learned for survival. Surely, no one had actually trained me for such a time. It was simply ingrained in me from childhood. I was taught a lot about money and credit and other things you do as a responsible adult, but evading the cop's questions and hiding assets were things I picked up *not* from words, but by having observed actions. Little did I realize, I was learning to hold my family secrets and evade questions so that I could elude and not acknowledge the true source of our family's wealth.

"What do your parents do?"

This was a question often asked by curious friends and associates because of the immense spending and vehicles I was seen being picked up in after school. I guess I learned early on that it was best to have an answer at the ready, to distract those who could cause harm or trouble by providing plausible answers. Regardless, many of my classmates never asked, either because they themselves grew up wealthy or they just couldn't believe that an ordinary Black kid from Detroit had parents who ran a quarter-of-a-billion-dollar drug empire.

Telling my story now has caused discomfort, as it feels totally the opposite of my core beliefs or how I spent most of my upbringing. Growing up shrouded in mystery, talking about what my parents did, or revealing the fact that my father was in prison, these were unspoken taboos. Guys I had grown up with wouldn't share with me that their father or parents were in the streets, or in prison, until we began to tell our story in the hopes of combating the stigma and shame carried by those who believe most people will judge or avoid them altogether if it became known they had a parent in prison or who sold drugs.

In this high-octane drug-fueled story of ours, we found redemption and strength, where it seemed little was left. Once taking part in the destruction of our own communities, I hope to show there is a silver lining for anyone, especially the children of those incarcerated. I want them to know there is hope on the other side and with faith anything can be overcome. My tribulations and perspective are the lessons I was given when I was stripped bare of all the material and monetary things that had made my family and me who we were—or so we had thought.

The millions of incarcerated individuals—Black, Brown, White, Yellow, and so on—serving time in state or federal prisons aren't the only ones who suffer from this nationwide epidemic. The ones who suffer the most are the children and the family left on the outside who must pick up the pieces and repair what's left. The silent victims of rising poverty—resulting from the connected impact of social and economic inequality in America—are riding in the passenger seats of their incarcerated loved ones' lives, and that leaves little hope for change.

—*Harold Corey Mills*

# BLACK MAFIA QUEEN

# Chapter 1

# A Storm Is Coming

*Victorville, California, 2008*

"WHERE AM I?"

With my head throbbing from a night of drinking, smoking marijuana, and partying too hard, I woke up to a blood- and piss-stained mattress staring back at me held up by the metal bars of my bunk. Wrapped in sheets that felt as thin as toilet paper on top of a beat-up lumpy old mattress, I looked around to see a dozen or so more bunks just like it, all lined in a row down a long, narrow dormitory. I closed my eyes once more, hoping it was all just a dream, when suddenly . . .

"Count time!" a man's voice announced through the intercom system.

Still, I remained with my head and face covered in a blanket, while my new roommates shuffled and moved around me, whispering about the new girl who had just arrived.

"Hey, hey." I felt a light tap on my side as I fought hard to keep my eyes closed and remain still.

"It's count time, you have to get up."

My eyelids clamped down tighter, resisting. I resented the tone

1

of concern in her voice and despised the care in her touch. Knowing I had no choice, I opened my eyes and pulled back the tattered blanket to see a pretty young Hispanic girl, with her jet-black hair slicked back into a ponytail, staring back at me.

"Come on, we have to line up for count," she said to me.

Still dreary and disoriented, I slowly pulled myself up and slipped into my standard-issue pumpkin-seed shoes. One by one, we all walked out and stood in a straight line along a long corridor that connected to several other dormitory-style rooms. Suddenly three guards charged through the threshold. A female guard, with dark sunglasses and a headcounter, clicked away; while a tall white male guard counted each prisoner out loud. The last one, an older white overweight gentleman, trailed just behind, keeping a close watch of things.

"Forty-three!" *CLICK* . . . "Forty-four!" . . . *CLICK*.

The click of the hand counter pierced my eardrum like the tick on a hand watch counting down until they had finally gotten to me. "Fifty-seven!" *CLICK* . . .

The counting and clicking would finally end and the group of girls would quickly disperse, heading in their separate directions, returning to whatever mundane task or conversation they were having before being abruptly interrupted and into their assigned bunks. Lost, and in a deep haze of emotion, I went back and crawled into my cold bunk.

"So, you new here?" asked the dark-haired Latina girl.

"Yeah, where you coming from?" another voice would answer and chime in from behind.

"*Coming from?*" I repeated back. It seemed like an unusual question to ask. "*Coming from?* Coming from home!" I quipped.

"Oh . . . you turned yourself in!" my new friend said in astonishment, while simultaneously answering her own question.

"I'm Maria," she blurted out with an eagerness to get to know her new bunkmate.

"And I'm Angie," the girl behind me remarked.

# A STORM IS COMING

I only pulled the blanket over my head tighter, hoping it would be a silent signal that I wasn't interested in getting to know them. My eyes remained closed, and I prayed that it would all end soon. I asked God to make this nightmare fall away. Clenching my jaws tighter, I could feel the wrinkles on the sides of my eyes grow more creased as I wished it all away. The room seemed to shrink more with every word they uttered.

"What they get you for?" Maria asked, breaking my train of thought.

My head only throbbed more. Thoughts swirled, my stomach twisted into knots, the sensation of feeling closed in only grew more foreboding. I began to feel hot, whipping the covers away. The words "I gotta get out!" seemed to fly from my mouth on their own; and in total disregard to her question, I jumped up.

Alarmed, Maria looked on, with a quizzical expression across her face. "You can't go anywhere!" she blurted out, as if I had forgotten I was in federal prison, and this wasn't some camp or rehab that I could leave at free will.

"Yeah, you don't want to go out there," Angie replied.

"I just gotta get out. I have to see what's out there."

"It's a sandstorm, you can't see anything," Maria replied.

Ignoring their warnings, I hopped out of bed and slipped back into my pumpkin-seed shoes.

"Go on . . . let her go out there," a big Black girl, with dark spots across her face, whose bunk sat in the far back corner of the room, said coldly. Her icy tone had little concern and interest in me, coupled with the fact it only seemed to dare me.

Apparently, "Blackie" was the name she earned while out running the streets as a young girl—it stemmed from her dark appearance and large frame. She was loud, boisterous, and downright mean. She wasn't the type of woman who got played with, and I did know a little too well how the streets had hardened her and forced her into being the bitch she was.

I wouldn't let any warnings stop me from going outside. I didn't care if it was a hurricane waiting just on the other side of the steel doors, I was going to have to just face it and see for myself. The road trip up to this hellhole was already a blur, while my arrival was spotty at best. I not only wanted to see my surroundings, but needed to see. I rushed out of our dorm and swiftly down the corridor toward the exit.

Pushing through the threshold, I emerged on the other side. The strong gust of wind swiftly slapped me across my face, then pushed and pulled at my clothes. I gazed around at my bleak surroundings in despair, and I could feel my own pity at the pit of my stomach. There were no beautiful trees, with long branches of leaves, or lush green grass covering the grounds; there were no flowers and beautiful shrubbery, not even any pesky weeds that needed to be hacked and pulled. There wasn't one speck of greenery; just bare dirt, rocks, and sand covered the land, except for a few bungalow-style buildings sprawled across the grounds. The sand clouds began to form, enveloping the sun and blue sky in a blanket of gray. It was hopeless to see even a few yards into the distance. Except for the menacing guard tower that peeked from behind the curtain of misery as a reminder. Just short of there was the men's facility, which would appear on clear days.

This was it. I had reached the bottom of my hole. I found a seat on the one single bench placed on the bare grounds and began to recall a recurring dream that terrorized me many nights leading up to this very moment. For weeks on end, I'd wake up in a cold sweat from an ongoing scene of me driving alone, speeding faster and faster to no particular destination, down a dark pathway toward a manhole that would emerge in the distance. I was forced to watch as the hole grew larger, as I drew closer, until I dived straight into it. Falling into a dark, bottomless pit terrorized my thoughts and left me with a knot in my stomach. Bewildered and confused, I didn't understand what it could mean, or where it was coming from, until now.

# A STORM IS COMING

*"Do you see this as where your life is heading?"* the voice of a high-priced Beverly Hills therapist echoed in my head.

Long before I found myself sitting on a bench in federal prison, contemplating those words, I had sought the help of a professional to help me find the cause of those dreams. I shrugged it off in denial of the inevitable. I lived the façade of an incredible life and hadn't begun to address the hard truth that it would eventually come crashing down and I would end up here. In the middle of nowhere, in the midst of a sandstorm. Something I'd only seen in movies.

It was hopeless to see anything, never mind my exact location. As if we were in the middle of the desert, the land definitely gave the impression that we were the only ones around, for miles to come. The thick sand clouds made it impossible to see just a few short yards in the distance; and without the blue sky to determine distance, it was a complete waste to even take a guess at how far the nearest form of civilization was. It felt like I was sitting in the middle of an abandoned field somewhere in the Mojave Desert. Tumbleweeds brushed past my feet, only to sink me lower. As I watched one bounce and roll, envy rushed through my veins. How free this ball of branches was, bouncing freely through the land without restriction or regret. Grief laden, I journeyed farther out, hoping the wind would take me away like the weeds that rolled past me.

Victorville Federal Camp didn't have any two gates or any guard towers. The desolation and the sheer bareness of the grounds, I assumed, were enough to strike fear in our hearts, to deter any of us from trying to leave; besides, most who made it to camp were serving short sentences, or were at the tail end of a lengthy one, and were highly unlikely to risk the chance of getting caught and sent off to a higher-security prison. Not that it mattered much, but I wondered how many women were here before me.

I've always hated math and can't live without a calculator, but I couldn't help but try to figure out how many days were left. Fifty-six months, twelve months in a year, how many times could twelve divide evenly into fifty-six? My brain seemed to jump from number to number, without any real sense or correlation. There were 365 days in a year, so for at least a thousand-something nights, I would have to return to that bunk. These were my thoughts as the sand caressed my face. With a deep breath, I took one last look at my surroundings before retreating.

The following day, I finally awoke in a calm mental state to find myself alone. My fellow bunkmates had already awoken and headed out on their daily routines, leaving me behind to find my own way. Just at my feet, I found someone had left a small tube of toothpaste, a toothbrush, and soap. Thankfully, someone knew that the first thing I would want to do is wash the taste of yesterday from my teeth and gums. I found my way down to the showers, and in one of the small stalls, I quickly washed away the dirt and dust from the day before. I scrubbed my teeth, threw on my government-issued garments, and headed out onto the campus.

While I crossed down one of the many pathways, a Black male guard headed toward me. He was tall and muscular, with a dark complexion and handsome. I would have guessed he was in his mid-thirties, if not for the slight gray hairs on his head. He squinted as if not recognizing me from around here.

"New?"

"Yes," I replied.

He chuckled. "Oh, okay, what's your name?"

"Toni."

"What's somebody like you doing here, Toni?"

I shyly put my head down, unable to think of what to say. Clearly, I had done something to end up here.

"OWEE!" He shook his head. "Well . . . you gonna have a hard time here."

I looked up at him, unable to understand what he meant as he gazed at me and smiled, still shaking his head. "Well, if you ever have any questions, you can let me know. I'm Officer Clark."

"What do you mean by 'a hard time'?"

He shifted back and forth, and appeared to begin to speak before taking a moment. "Ah, you just got a look. A look these women around here not gone like."

Blankly I looked at him, as if silently searching for a clarification in his facial expression.

"You're just a good-looking woman. These ladies around here have a hard time with that. It's best you stay on the up and up around here, lest you end up in one of their crosshairs." He shrugged as if getting some heavy secret off his chest. "They can make it hard for you in here. I've seen a lot of ladies like you come and go, and it all depends on how you deal with them that determines how you leave here."

Startled, I felt chills down my spine from his honesty. Just before getting settled in, I had already received the first warning that something as shallow as the way I looked would cause me trouble and would put my freedom in jeopardy.

"You get assigned a job yet?"

"No," I muttered, distracted by the thought of these women who could cause me trouble.

"Well, you should go down to the job coordinator and get assigned before you end up in the warehouse."

"Warehouse?" I replied flatly.

"Yeah, you don't want that job. It's dirty and hard. You'll have to carry and move things around all day. You'll hate it."

I thanked him for forewarning me before making my way down to the chow hall. The first meal was a simple turkey meat sandwich with cheese, chips, an apple, and juice. I rejoined Maria and some of the other girls from the bunk; they were seated under the shade at an outside picnic table.

"Did you get assigned a job yet?" Maria asked.

I shook my head as I bit into the dry sandwich, washing it down with the apple-cranberry juice they served with the meal.

"Girl, you better hope they don't put you in the warehouse," Joseline blurted out from across the table. Joseline was an older, light-skinned Dominican woman, who was just about at the tail end of a twenty-five-year sentence for drug conspiracy.

*"Warehouse,"* I repeated with more concern after hearing the warning about this job again.

"Yeah, you should try to get the kitchen or something. You should go soon, before you end up there," Maria said without understanding that I still had no idea what the warehouse job was. I just knew that after all of this, I definitely didn't want to find out why everyone dreaded the warehouse so much. I felt a pit in my stomach as I got worried about the prospect of ending up with this job assignment.

"They gon' give her the warehouse job, that's the only one with any openings," Blackie replied, almost as if chiming in to only make me sink even lower into my seat. I couldn't bear the thought of any more torture and grueling demands. It's like she knew it would affect me, almost like pricking me with a needle if only to see if I'd squeal.

"I'm not working at the warehouse!" I shot back with an utter certainty that even shocked me. How could I be so sure?

*God got me,* I thought.

"I'll be fine," I said aloud, without giving Blackie or anyone else the impression that I was worried or scared of the implications of ending up in the warehouse or any other dreadful job assignment no one wanted. I quickly finished the bitter-tasting apple and scarfed down the rest of my sandwich before getting up from the table and trotting away.

I found my way down the courtyard into one of the administrative buildings, where I found job coordinator Malcolm Joe tucked away in his office. He was grappling with a stack of paper-work that sat at his desk. I knocked on the door and he quickly ushered me in.

"New here?"

"Yes," I replied shyly as I moved closer. He waved toward the two chairs facing opposite him at his desk.

"Here, have a seat. Name?"

I swiftly took a seat and took in my surroundings. He appeared to be a newlywed; there were several photos of him and a bride framed and hung on the wall behind him.

"Welch, Tonesa Welch . . ."

He slid over in his chair to face the computer and typed into the keyboard. "You got any preference where you want to be or anything you good at?"

"Uh," I answered, startled by the question. I could hardly think fast enough at any desirable job I could possibly choose. Nothing came to mind, except all the jobs the other ladies detested—least of all, the warehouse. *Just not the warehouse,* I thought. Hesitant, I feared voicing my concerns, thinking it would only incite him to punish me with the strenuous assignment.

"We don't have many openings around here, actually," Malcolm Joe said. He clicked and clacked a few more keys on his keyboard. "I'm gone put you in the warehouse. They got some openings down there."

My stomach suddenly sank to the bottom of my body. It just seemed to get worse and worse. I was already dealing with my new living situation, and now I had the worst job on campus. It was like a dreadful cloud hung over me and I could hear the girls saying they told me so. Defeated, I lifted out of my chair and headed for the door. *I just won't tell them,* I thought as I reached for the doorknob. More dread struck as I imagined the smirk on Blackie's face from being right.

"You know what!" Malcolm exclaimed just as I pulled open the door.

Quickly I turned to face Malcolm, who stood brushing his lips with his index finger, as if in deep thought. "I'm gone put you in the chapel. Yeah, I'm gone put you in the chapel," he repeated, maybe just to hear himself come up with an amazing alternative. He agreed with his decision and swiftly moved back over to the computer and typed. Just then, I strongly believe, God Himself had come down and whispered into his ear that there was a better use for me.

# Chapter 2
# How Did I Get Here?

I N THE PRISON CHAPEL, IT WAS JUST ME, MY MOP, AND GOD. I'D COME a long way from my weekly $20,000 shopping sprees. It was a long drive from Rodeo Drive to the women's federal prison camp in Victorville, California. Ironically, I wore designer clothes to my self-surrender at the prison camp—my last tie to the high life I had been living.

And *POOF!*

As soon as my expensive clothes were stripped from me during the strip search, then placed in a garbage bag for safekeeping until my release years later, any last physical reminder of that high life was gone in an instant. I had unwillingly exchanged Prada for the puke-green prison smock I was now wearing. My well-kept hands had gone from gripping the steering wheel of a $200,000 Aston Martin to clutching the handle of a $20 mop.

Before that time, my relationship with God was . . . let's just say . . . spotty at best. It's hard to think of God when there's so much Gucci to be bought and worn! However, spending hours a day in that lonely chapel (God wasn't too popular with the women in prison) mopping up, I had plenty of time to ponder my relationship with the Almighty. Over time, it became clear to me that

11

He had designed a divine plan to get me all alone with Him in that chapel.

The chapel was a normal room, with some pews in it. I hadn't had much of a relationship with God before spending time there. The extent of my relationship with God was a typical one of praying to Him when I wanted things to go my way—that was about it. But in this fluorescent-lit prison chapel, I felt His presence. Outside the doors were the noise, the fights, the guards, and the yelling. Behind the doors, it was just me and Him.

Near the chapel was the office of a prison psychologist, Sam, who ran the prison drug treatment and therapy programs. He was a kind man—one of the only bright spots that could be found in the prison, and I wanted to speak to him. However, Sam told me he wasn't allowed to have conversations with inmates in his office, unless they were formally part of one of the programs he administered.

I didn't let that stop me, so I devised a plan to get into his office to talk with him more. I noticed that his office wasn't clean. The trash bin wasn't being emptied often enough, and the floor needed a good mopping—which was now my specialty.

"Can I clean your office?" I asked Sam. I guess he figured that an inmate assigned to cleaning duty near his office was allowed inside, so he nodded yes, and let me in.

I found myself there often because Sam Woods and Torrie Andrews seemed like two of the hipper members of the system. Sam was a Black guy from Kansas, or somewhere like that, who had just returned from a tour of duty in Iraq and had now taken a job as a prison psychologist. Torrie was a girl who bent gender rules and had this masculine aura about her. They were both cool and welcoming from the day I walked in, and it gave me this comfort to come and talk to them. Sam seemed like someone I may have grown up with. He was smart and knew a lot about the hip-hop scene and what was going on outside the walls. He seemed wise beyond his years and would often help put things into perspective for me.

One day, when I was in there mopping, he asked me, "Why do you always look so unhappy?"

My transformation that came about during my fifty-seven months in prison—partly through Sam's help—hadn't washed over me yet. I still had a constant scowl on my face.

"Um . . . because I'm in prison . . ." I responded.

"Well, why do you think you're here?" Sam asked.

"Because Terry and Meech got me into this life."

My statement that Terry and Meech "got me into this life" was bullshit. A part of me knew it, but mopping those floors, instead of cleaning up the goods on the showroom floor of Louis Vuitton with my wads of cash, and sleeping in a cot in a prison dorm, instead of a king-sized bed in my Mulholland Drive mansion, had me looking for someone to blame.

Over many months, Sam got me to see that I had no one to blame but myself. "You were hustling cocaine for decades before you got tangled up with the Flenory brothers," Sam pointed out. While it was easy to bullshit myself, it was hard to bullshit a guy who had access to detailed court records and confessions from my guilty plea. Sam's main gift to me was that he held a mirror up to the bullshit coming out of my mouth. I had no choice but to look at myself straight in the mirror.

Sam had just finished several tours in the Iraq war. "Trust me, I see where you're at, and it ain't nothing compared to being in Iraq," he said, shaking his head after one of my many complaints. "I spent years out there—eating food not much better than here, sleeping on beds not much better, showering in similar circumstances, while wearing tons of gear in one-hundred-plus–degree weather. And on top of all that, we had to worry about not getting killed," he said.

Sometimes it seemed as though he was cutting into me. How could I think about how hard of a time I was having, when there were countless kids like him going to war and grappling with the thought of death looming at every corner?

"See, all you gotta do is not get into no trouble for the next few years and you're out of here!" he said, giving me tough love and a reality check. "Imagine not knowing if a sniper is waiting for you to come from the shadows, or wondering if the next step you take could be the last. Nothin' worse than that. No shit compares to wondering if you'll make it another twenty-four hours, day in and day out." He would say this blankly, as if he wouldn't accept any other logical argument.

His words cut through me and opened my mind to consider what he was trying to convey to me. I could believe it was some psych trick he was playing on me, as I began to feel pangs of guilt if I got down on myself or upset about my surroundings. Sam made me open my eyes to understand this wasn't a punishment from God, but a message to reflect and seek understanding. I had spent the last decade of my life headed on a crash course straight to turmoil, and this was now the time to turn things around. I just had to get through these months, and I would be out to restart my life and do things the right way, the second time around.

"I'm going to help you get in the drug program. That will be the fastest way for you to get out of here," Sam said one day during one of our lengthy conversations.

A feeling of relief and excitement rushed over me when I heard him reassure me that he would get me a place in the prison drug program. The drug program was reserved for those the prison board felt could benefit from help with addiction and prevent them from returning on similar offenses. The program would also shave eighteen months off the sentence of anyone who completed it successfully. It already had a long waiting list and strict selection process, while those who were given consideration were known as heavy abusers. Pointing to my drunken deliriousness when I turned myself in, Sam argued that I was a strong candidate for the program and believed that I could set an example for the other ladies.

His words would echo in my head over and over throughout my time there. "Stop being so bitter, you can't spend your whole life mad at everyone for the mistakes *you* made."

"I know," I replied, but it was easier said than done. It seemed impossible that I was the only one to blame. All the talking my boyfriend did on cell phones, the billboards and videos his brother put up, or the Grammy-winning producer who told on me . . . these must have been the reasons I was in jail. Not to mention my own family who sat idly by and watched as I stuck my hand in the cookie jar one too many times. They let me risk my freedom so they could enjoy all the benefits that came with it—shopping trips, vacations, cars, and money whenever they needed it. I did it all, and in the end, I felt used and thrown away when only a handful checked on me and made sure I was good, now that all the fun times had ended and I couldn't bail them out of a jam whenever they wanted. Sam slowly helped me break down that bitterness and understand my own role in how my life was turning out.

*DIIIIIINNNNNGGGGGGGGGG!*
The loud morning bell began to ring out signaling the count time, waking me up for another day of work at the prison chapel. Once again, we'd all stand in line as the guards counted each of us, one by one, before all the ladies would scramble out of the bungalow to head toward their jobs. My heart felt heavy, considering that I was still adjusting to this being my life for the next few years. Bitter and upset, I still felt pangs of guilt. On the one hand, I had dodged the dreadful obligation of the warehouse; yet I was still resentful for being assigned to the chapel. My thoughts

would race with anger at Terry, his brother, the leeches, and all the other users who helped get me here. If it wasn't for any of them, I would still be free, or so I told myself.

Now as I started my bid, I would be sent to a place that I had partially lost faith in. I spent many days driving and dragging Terry, along with the rest of the family, from our Bel-Air home to South Central Los Angeles to hear Reverend Blake speak—only for all the countless words of the day and praising we did in the house of the Lord to amount to nothing. It was impossible not to see how bitter I had become.

"Do you believe in God, Toni?" Pastor Arnold had asked when I first arrived at the chapel.

"Absolutely," I replied, still unsure of just how much I believed at the time.

"Well, this chapel here is for all religions, whether you are Christian, Buddhist, or any other faith." Pastor Arnold was an older white guy, with a full head of gray hair and a bright smile.

"Come, let me pray for you." He had led me to kneel just before the cross in the front of the room and quietly prayed for me, almost as if in a whisper only he, God, and I could hear.

"I just need you to tidy up around here and make sure you sweep and polish the floors. Once you get done, I won't make much of a fuss," he whispered.

"I can do that," I replied.

"Good, I'm sure if God chose for you to be here, it was for a good reason." He had smirked and glided away, leaving me to look at the room, which had a few pews, while the walls were lined with quotes about faith and bulletins about how to manage anger and depression.

The chapel was one of the less-visited areas of the prison, and Pastor Arnold spent a lot of the time in his offices or off campus if he wasn't lecturing during Bible study or giving a service on Sundays. There wasn't much to be maintained; so after sweeping and dusting, I spent most days reading while on duty. My son Corey, along with several friends and family members, subscribed to magazines for me and sent books to my prison address, which provided me with a good amount of reading material.

There were women who had served ten, twenty, almost thirty years; so compared to what other girls had got caught up doing, and the time they received, I had gotten off lucky. Sam and Torrie would soon offer to protect me and back me up if the administrative ladies tried to stir up any troubles. Having been there for some time, they had seen some female prisoners end up in bad situations, getting time added to their sentences for misbehavior or petty jealousies from some of the counselors.

I guess I didn't realize what I was doing to myself. I began to read the Bible and explore other religions, reading excerpts from the Quran and the Torah in my free time after tidying up the chapel. The chapel and Sam would bring a reprieve to everyday prison life and open me up to questioning long-held beliefs and putting my life into perspective. When I first got to prison, I was sent to Victorville, a facility in the middle of nowhere in the California desert. I felt like I had just been dropped out of the sky onto these bleak surroundings, where I didn't understand how or why. I just kept asking God, "Why me?" until one day the question changed. I altered my outlook, and instead of asking, "Why me?" I would ask God, "How did I get here?"

# Chapter 3

# Little Brown Girl

*Detroit, 1961 to 1978*

N O, PUT IT BACK . . ." MY MOM WOULD SAY WITHOUT PAUSE. SHE had no qualms about using the word "no"—ever. Since an early age, I had always been deeply interested in fashion and the latest trends. I was so consumed with fashion spreads and articles, like it was a job in and of itself. Up until I graduated from high school, my mother still bought my clothes and went shopping with me.

Every Friday after she'd get off from work, we'd head off to the mall and retail outlets. Our differing tastes in fashion were wide and far apart, to say the least, and she rarely picked things I liked, let alone things that I wanted. On the one hand, she didn't care much about clothes or following the latest trends, while I gravitated toward big-name designer duds and high-quality materials, which were way above and beyond her Ford Motor Company salary and my own means.

"Oh, Mom! Look at this dress!" I exclaimed one evening after slipping inside a boutique at the Northland Mall.

"Hmm, that's nice," she bemoaned. "Now, how much is it?"

Looking down at the price tag, I saw it was several hundred dollars.

"*Oh, nooo!* Put it back," she ordered.

"But—" I protested.

"When you get a job, you can buy whatever you like," she quipped with a snigger, and without saying another word, she slipped out of the boutique. Regardless, we formed a strong bond from our girl time; and I undoubtedly would still find items she approved of and would fit into what she was comfortable spending with her hard-earned cash.

There's no doubt I got my love of fashion and shopping from my mother. She was dubbed "Mall Lady" by her best friend and cousin, my aunt Delores. It was the moniker the rest of the family and her friends would quickly adopt and know her by. Although we frequented the mall regularly, my mother was conservative and never spent beyond her means. Despite her finding joy in shopping, I believe it was her way of dealing with and masking her sadness of being in an unfaithful marriage.

I was born as a result of a short fling between my mother, Carol Thomas, and my father, OD Banks. I guess my mother spent some time after my two brothers' father was murdered to explore and winded up meeting OD. They would commence a torrid love affair, while he was already married to my stepmother, Rose. Needless to say, the union was fated to fail, and I was conceived out of this hapless arrangement. Eventually she would go on to marry my stepfather, Emerson Thomas, in 1972. They would have one child together, my youngest brother, Kevin, and remained married until his death in the summer of 2013.

Although I had a seemingly good childhood, I always felt disconnected from the rest of my family. Not only was I the only girl out of three boys, but my appearance was notably different from the rest of the brood as well. My brothers were light-skinned, with light eyes, and had all the charm in the world. I had typical brown skin and eyes. I thought my mother doted on the boys, while she was strict and demanding when it came to me. Eventually I grew to understand that it was her way of showing she expected more from me and knew I was stronger than the boys. Although, at the time, it was hard not to feel I got the short end of the stick. My stepfather, Emerson, never seemed to let me forget it.

"Tonesa! You as dark as me!" he'd spit out in his old Southern drawl. "Pops," as we would all grow to call him, always had one more joke up his sleeve and poked fun at everyone. He had a wise-crack for everything, and his heavy Alabama accent and hearty chuckle endeared him to everyone who crossed his path. Except for me, of course; I couldn't stand him. I could remember days just wishing he would leave. I didn't care if he wound up behind some dumpster on the east side of Detroit or ran off with some younger woman—all I knew was I wanted him gone.

"People gone think you adopted," I would remember him saying.

I chalked it up to jealously on my stepfather's behalf, oblivious to the fact that I served as a reminder of his long-held rivalry with my biological father and even a bruise to his ego. OD and Emerson had seemingly been running mates and hung around the same circles. Surely, there was some unspoken rivalry between the two, and my mom was in the dead center of it.

One day out of the blue, Emerson started talking about my dad. He chided me about how OD got beat up by my eldest brother's father. I could feel myself shrinking as my brothers joined in, joking, laughing, and teasing me. It would be a short while before I even knew my father—what he looked or even sounded like, but his absence left a sharp gap in my being. He nicknamed me "Darkie," while totally ignorant of his own skin color. He even had the audacity to exclaim, "Toni, you're the blackest one in the house!"

He came from the country and it was clear he was taught to hate his own skin color. Even though I knew he was darker than I was, I would come to believe him. He got my brothers to join in and they'd come up with a song together, "Darkie, darkie, darkie," singing in tandem. I would just cry, the feeling of helplessness rushing over me. There was nowhere for me to go or no one to run to. It would become so ingrained in my head that I was dark. As I got older, when people would tell me I was light and not as dark as I thought, I wouldn't believe them.

I remember some days just as his car would pull up into the driveway after a long day at the plant, I would hop from the windowsill and hide in the closet. It was one of those closets where your parents put all the random things that they didn't want to sit out. Ours was just that, a closet full of junk and old stuff we didn't need or hardly used anymore. I can still recall how I went so far back, no one could find me there. I would go curl up and hide away from his ridicule and jokes and spend many days there in my own little fashion world. As I grew into my teenage years, I still held on to these hang-ups, not feeling confident in myself.

My biological dad would finally appear somewhere around the time I was nine years old. By this time, we were living on Coyle Street, on the West Side of Detroit. I can still remember how my mom had dressed me in a really pretty dress, and he came to the porch. He was a short, dark, handsome man wearing a baseball cap and was dressed well. The joy at seeing his smiling face made me feel so warm, like I finally belonged to someone after my brother Darry had led me to believe he found me in a dumpster somewhere. It was a nice summer day as we walked down Coyle Street. Kids were out playing as the parents hung out on their porches watching us as we walked by. My father didn't drive, so we made our way down to the bus stop to start a long trek over to the east side.

On the way, I asked a bunch of questions like, "What does the *O* and *D* stand for in your name?"

To my surprise, it didn't stand for anything.

"That's it, just OD Banks," he answered, chuckling.

"No middle name and nothing else to it," he replied with such a cool tone. Unlike Emerson, my father was laid back and quiet, for the most part. He carried a certain cool factor, like one of those jazz musicians back in the day who didn't let anything get to them. On the bus, he told me about his wife and the rest of his family and how I'd get to meet my other sisters and brothers.

When we finally arrived at his house, I would meet his wife, Rose. It was sometime in August, around my birthday, so she had affectionately baked me a cake. I met Jackie and Kim, my sisters. We were close in age, so we got along well and would play together. My dad had a big family, and now all of a sudden, I had one, too. During the day while he and my stepmom worked, we would go over to my aunt's house. I don't remember too much about her other than she watched subunits. Those visits quickly turned unpleasant after she gathered the rest of the kids and told them to watch how she'd beat her children, using me as the guinea pig. She wanted me to cry, but I wouldn't. All I felt was anger, which I would hold on to until the day she died. She thought it was funny, but her laughter ceased when she realized she couldn't make me cry.

My dad would finally return to retrieve us, and Kim would tell him what happened. He didn't do a thing, not even flinch. It was like he didn't care at all. He stayed quiet as we walked back, and that feeling came rushing back over me. I had no one to help me. Just like at home with Emerson, no one cared how I felt, nor was anyone willing to come to my rescue. After that, I wouldn't see my father until years later.

I was left to endure more of Emerson's berating and teasing. I think to him poking and prodding me was just as satisfying as getting at the man who made me. From the time I woke up for school, until I got ready for bed, he'd berate me about how I cleaned the dishes, but didn't dry and put them away, to some other minuscule detail that only left most of us baffled. He used his mouth as if it were a gun, and I happened to be his target practice. Emerson would hurl barbs at me that he instinctively knew would break me.

Finally, one evening, once we were a little older, Darry, who had become fed up with his treatment, intervened. Darry was the second oldest of my brothers, with fair skin and the lightest green eyes.

"Tonesa, Tonesa, get down here!" Emerson shrieked from the living room.

I reluctantly came down the stairs and saw him standing in the doorway, where he began to ream me in, as he would usually do.

"Stop it!" Darry yelled as he ran in. "You gone leave her alone . . . I said stop it, damn it!"

I had never seen Darry get so loud or have so much anger toward Emerson before. His face was beet red, and his hands were balled into a fist. The look on Emerson's face was of pure shock! It appeared as if he could almost fall over.

"Now I done had enough of you talking to her that way!" Darry went on. The stern sound in his voice gave us both pause.

Startled, Emerson seemed to take a few minutes to process what Darry was saying. It was unmistakable by the rage in my brother's eyes that he'd had enough and was ready to fight, if it came to that and Emerson didn't stop chiding me. After that incident, Emerson didn't bother me so much anymore, and I largely avoided his crosshairs as much as I possibly could.

In time, I would grow closer to my brothers, despite our obvious differences. My adolescence was spent as a tomboy chasing them around, hopping fences, climbing trees, or whatever else they would challenge me to do. Just because I was little and a girl didn't mean I couldn't do it—and sure enough, I would prove it . . . scars, cuts, and bruises later. That's probably where I got my first sense of rebellion. Keeping up with the guys sometimes meant breaking the rules and going against our parents' wishes and rules. It was all in good fun, and Ernest and especially Darry kept a keen interest in my well-being.

No matter what time of the day or side of town I was on, Darry would come running at the first sign of trouble. He was my protector, my best friend, and my own guardian. I attribute a lot of who I am because of him, and he's the reason for my inclination to hang around guys more often than women. Over time, he would teach me how to ride a bike, swim, defend myself, and many other things before getting mixed up with drugs leading to his murder one cold October morning.

While both my older brothers were notable womanizers, Ernest especially took an interest in wooing the ladies and having some of the craziest parties when our parents were away. He was very popular among our peers, and the girls swooned over him. It would be through him that I would meet the father of my firstborn, Marlon McFarlin. Shortly after graduating, Ernest took a job at the Ford plant and quickly sparked a friendship with Ricky, Marlon's brother. Whenever Ernest, Ricky, and their girlfriends would party and hang out, Marlon would tag along, and we sparked up a friendship, which later led to dating and eventually living together.

Hardly the prom-queen type, I spent most of my teenage and high school years as an outcast goody-two-shoes. Most of the girls didn't like me and the guys were uninterested, and reasonably so, as my small, undeveloped frame paled in comparison to some of the more developed girls, like my childhood friends Wendy and Jazz. In high school, all of the guys hounded them because they had the bodies, boobs, and butts. While I had to be careful that I didn't "fly away in a storm because you're so skinny," Pops once joked. As I browsed through the pages of my parents' *Ebony* and *Jet* magazines, I saw skinny girls just like me wearing the latest fashions and trends, and I wanted to rock all of that clothing, too.

After meeting Marlon at the end of my tenth-grade year, all I could think about was graduating and getting out on my own.

Marlon was older and had already graduated, with plans to attend college in Oklahoma. You couldn't tell me anything; I thought I had it all figured out in my last years of high school. Here I was, with this older guy who had plans for the future, while these girls were all dating the same boys we went to class with.

Marlon hardly had himself together back then. I can remember him coming to pick me up for prom, plastered and sloppy drunk, and the car he planned to chauffeur me in was filthy. I couldn't believe it. Devastated, I bolted into the house, up the stairs, and into the bathroom of our family home on Coyle Street, concerned about our cream ensemble being ruined by the dusty exterior. I cried into the mirror, before my mom came in and re-assured me not to worry, and how I would soon forget all about this stupid guy who ruined such an important time in my life. Not exactly forgetting it or him, like she said I would, but eventually I'd hardly be able to retell the tale without a hearty chuckle.

Dating Marlon was a package deal. He came with a host of sis-ters, brothers, and other close relatives, who would become and remain my family, even to this day. When all the boys started hanging, Marlon brought his sister Robin around and we became thicker than thieves. Blood couldn't have made us any closer; and while the boys would head off to drink and do whatever it was they did, Robin and I conceived our own mischief and plotted ways to come across a dollar. We would do almost anything and everything, except objectify or sell our bodies, for money. We shoplifted, passed off fake bills, and did every other petty crime under the sun. Despite having gotten my first job at sixteen, I never stopped thinking about how I could make just a little extra money so I could get that Gucci pair of shoes or Fendi bag I had been eyeing in the latest *Vogue* magazine.

I wanted to wear these things—I needed to have the latest bags, shoes, and accessories. Almost like an addiction, my desire would only grow and worsen. When you're young, it's like you're invincible, the fear of consequences or the effect rarely crosses your mind. Now I wouldn't try half the things I did.

"Bitch, they never check for receipts at Marshalls, as long as you got the tags," I recall Robin saying as we headed down the highway one day. "I wear it and then take it back!" she exclaimed.

It's like a light bulb went off in my head the second after Robin said it. "So we could put some shit in our bag and then return it and get the money," I said dubiously.

She paused as if the idea had never occurred to her before adding, "Hell yeah! We should do it. We can go in, split up, and act like we're browsing. That way, they can't watch us both."

A part of me wants to say it was a joke, but here she was helping me plot this grand heist. Realistically, I knew it wouldn't make us any real money, but it was a start. From there, we would spend some weekends going to different stores and picking up a few extra items that didn't make it to the register, always buying some random item here and there to throw the salesgirl off. Sometimes we'd wear the things we lifted before returning it all for cash and use the extra funds to pay for recreational drugs, alcohol, and hanging out.

Unlike the rest of my family, after graduating high school, I did not work at the Ford Motor plant. Emerson was the first to work for one of the plants before pulling my mother in and eventually my two older brothers, Ernest and Darry. It wasn't as if I didn't try, though, but ultimately I would be led down a different path. After going through the process and filling out my application for a position at Ford, I was required to fulfill a health exam, which I would fail. I remember that day when I received the call that, unfortunately, due to a heart murmur, which the examining physician discovered, Ford Motor Company would not extend an offer of employment to me because of the many health risks it posed.

I soon moved to Oklahoma to be with Marlon. That couldn't have lasted more than three months. He had a small apartment on the campus of the college he was attending, and we attempted to settle into life, playing house as a couple. I felt miserable, there was barely anything to do in Oklahoma and I had no friends. Marlon spent most of his time either working or at school, and never had much time to do anything fun. Whenever he did have any free time, he spent most of it studying or nose-deep in some book. It just didn't feel right. My heart wasn't in it, as much as I thought it would be; and not even a month in, I longed to fly home.

Marlon was a great guy. He was smart and dedicated to his studies, but I felt a certain emptiness. Life in Oklahoma didn't feel right to me. I longed to do something different, big even. I just couldn't grapple with the slow pace of the small-town college life, and I wanted to be free. That didn't stop me, however, from conceiving my first child, Marlon Jr., with his father, and then I broke the news to him that I was moving back to Michigan to raise my son there, instead of a college campus with no family or friends.

# Chapter 4

# Revolving Door

*Detroit, 1982 to 1986*

I WAS HALFWAY DRESSED WHEN SOMEONE BEGAN TO KNOCK AT THE door. Quietly crossing over my small apartment's living room, I peered through the peephole. It was Carol.

Carol was one of my friends I'd met when I was fourteen. I knew her through my brother Darry's girlfriend DeeDee when they'd drive into the city from Inkster. I was slightly in awe of these girls because they were older and could dress their asses off. They took pride in what they wore, from the cute dresses and shoes to the bangles and necklaces they accessorized them with, and I yearned to be the same way. Soon after I moved back to the city and got my own apartment, Carol happened to live a few doors down. Now independent and on my own, we would hit the city often.

Carol was one of the first girls I knew who dated street dudes. We would go out and she'd introduce me to the cute friends of the guy she happened to be going with at the time. They were hustlers who dressed in fancy clothes, flashy jewelry, and drove nice cars. It was on nights like these that I would encounter some

28

of the most notorious hustlers Detroit has ever produced, from the Chambers brothers to "Maserati Rick." The latter one I could remember hounding me for a date on many occasions before his unfortunate and untimely death like so many others due to running around the streets raising hell.

Truthfully, there wasn't much time to spare between raising my son and work. Luckily, my mom would occasionally agree to babysit. Carol and I would get dressed up and hit the town. She liked to hit all the trendy, happening spots in the city, and whenever I could, I'd join right along. While she would dress up in these fancy coats and tote expensive bags around, I could hardly afford any of that stuff, so she'd let me borrow a pair of shoes or a purse so that I could fit in with all the other glitzy girls who hung around.

"Come on, girl, open up!" Carol yelled through the door.

"Hey!"

I opened the door to see Carol in a leather skirt and jacket ensemble, waiting.

"You ain't dressed?" she asked, shocked to see I was hardly dressed, since I told her I'd be ready an hour ago.

"Girl, you know I ain't got no clothes like that," I replied.

"Bullshit, what you got on is cute, but what are you gonna wear with it?"

"I know, but I don't got any shoes to go with it," I said, exasperated.

"I got some Guccis that would look good with that outfit. We can run down to my spot on the way out and grab them."

Once in her apartment, Carol pulled out some barely worn heels from a box in her closet.

"Perfect," I said as I checked myself out in the mirror one last time.

Carol snickered. "All right, come on, they are waiting on us."

We headed out the door and drove straight to Sinbad's to meet Pedro.

# BLACK MAFIA QUEEN

* * *

Sinbad's was this new, happening downtown place, located off Jefferson, near the docks, with a view of the Michigan lakes. Back then, it was the place to be. It would be packed with a line down the street on weekends, and you could hardly sit without a reservation. I can't remember if the food was any good; but if you were there, it meant you were somebody to know. All the hustlers and fly girls would bustle through the doors in their full-length minks, gator shoes, and tons of diamond and gold jewelry. They'd proceed to order endless amounts of alcohol and champagne. If you were looking to make a connection or hook up with a fly boy, this was the place to start.

Carol and I would come in and have drinks and dinner with whatever guy she was talking to at the time, and we'd move along to the next spot. Sometimes we would just party there. Sinbad's had a third floor that was mostly an all-dance area, with a huge fully stocked bar that sat in the middle, which would turn into a club on certain nights. I remember going and wanting to have some of the things all the other girls were wearing. I became enamored with the lifestyle all these guys and girls were living. They would come in with their posse and splurge on bottles of champagne, while dressed to the nines, with bright smiles on their faces as if nothing could touch them.

Pedro was a guy Carol had hit it off with and had just begun seeing. He was in the streets, but well put together. Pedro carried himself better than most and treated her well. When we got to Sinbad's, we glided through the doors and headed up the elevator right into the party. The music blasted from the speakers while the dance floor was packed with partygoers dancing the night away. We found seats near the bar.

"What y'all trying to drink?" Pedro asked.

Carol turned to me with a sly look in her eyes. "Champagne!" she said with assertiveness, laughing in her girlish giggle as she nudged me for support.

"Champagne would be good," I agreed.

Pedro didn't just order us two glasses of champagne, but the whole damn bottle. The bartender came and placed a bucket of ice in front of us before popping the cork on a chilled bottle of Perrier-Jouët and poured us both a glass.

"Cheers, bitch!" Carol said playfully as we clinked our glasses together in a toast, grinning the biggest schoolgirl smiles. Pedro would soon divert his attention from his boys that he came with and pull Carol onto the dance floor, where he would twirl her around and embrace her in his arms while the DJ spun. I was too shy and introverted to really mingle with anyone, so I hung back by the bar. I watched as some of the guys sat around and got at each other about street business while the women stood by.

Suddenly it was as if the crowd opened up or he just stepped right through. Standing on the opposite side of the dance floor was a tall, handsome light-skinned guy staring back at me. He was sharp-looking, dressed in nice gray slacks, a jacket, and a white button-up; I was instantly attracted. To me, he seemed different. He wasn't all flashy like the other guys—his style was understated and refined. Right then and there, I knew that I wanted him to be my man. He quickly crossed over the dance floor through the crowd, over to the bar where I was sitting.

"How you doin'? I'm Harold."

"I'm Toni," I said.

With all the charm in the world, he stretched his hand out to shake mine.

"Can I buy you a drink?"

I shrugged my shoulders while looking back at the bottle, which had swiftly been emptied. I had lost count of how many glasses I already had, but there was no way I was going to turn down this brother from ordering me another.

"Sure," I replied quickly.

It would be this chance encounter that set me on a completely different path and introduced me to a world where I had only sat on the outer fringes. Harold was a local dealer making a name for himself out on the East Side of Detroit. For all his subtle charm, he wasn't known for being the most compassionate guy on the street. Despite my intuition, and my inner voices piping up to tell me to steer clear of him, I was like a deer caught in headlights. I couldn't resist getting involved with this charming bad boy. He was handsome, had a good sense of style, and, on top of everything, was getting money and respect. Pedro knew him from around and they briefly ran in the same circle and now we would all hang together.

At the time, Harold was by no means rich or a big-time drug dealer, but he was obviously on his way and soon we would become a team. He would commission me to run little errands for him, here and there; and I, in turn, would introduce him to some of the guys I knew from the West Side. The East Side was known to be rougher and more beaten down than the West, while those on the East were easily distrustful of those from the West, and neither side crossed the border onto either side without good reason. Harold was from the East Side, so he avoided the West as much as possible, and I quickly became that bridge for him.

Harold was like the fire and I the lighter fluid. In good times, we made each other better; in bad times, it was like we both could make a situation ten times worse. I was wild and daring in comparison to his more reserved demeanor. I would routinely push his buttons and dare him to try riskier things, which he would reluctantly try.

"I got something!" I said slyly one day while we prepared to hit a party.

While he headed down the road, I reached into my purse and pulled out a small bag of little crystal rocks.

"What the hell is that?" he asked.

"H, ain't never seen crack before?" I quipped with a look of joking disbelief.

# REVOLVING DOOR

Crack was just starting to hit in the 1980s and it was everywhere. Up until meeting Harold, I had never done any drugs outside of alcohol. Soon after having met him, he introduced me to his world. He would bring rolled-up joints of marijuana; he'd teach me how to break down lines of coke. This opened me up to experiment with whatever other drug I could get my hands on. He would bring one thing, and I would go out and find something stronger.

Despite our apparent penchant for doing drugs and partying, Harold and I also shared a common interest in making money and wearing designer clothes. He would eventually buy me some of my first designer bags and shoes. While he spent his day out on the streets hustling, I would head to work and return home to care for Marlon, but that didn't stop me from wanting to be involved.

"I know some guys interested in getting some of that stuff you have."

He would sit quietly as I pitched him on a potential customer he could connect with, before reluctantly replying, "Yeah, all right. Yeah."

To avoid an argument or debate, he'd get up and head out the door with me. Just like with Robin, I was always itching to be involved in something to make a few extra dollars. Doubt or fear never crossed my mind back in those days. While Harold would sit and ponder the outcomes of things, I would already be racing to do it and pulling him right along with me. He would pitch a fit and, in the end, always without a doubt, follow my direction or advice. He, in turn, would teach me how to bag up nickel and dime bags and I'd sell them to some of the girls that we hung with.

I wasn't the little girl whose mom bought her clothes anymore. I couldn't just go back to who I once was. It was way too late for that. I got my taste of the life and wanted more. It was just like I got this high out of living life on the edge, breaking rules, and

33

getting away with it. While money would be my reasoning behind most of it, the high that came with it was the true motivator—a sensation that leaves every nerve ending tingling as the blood rushes from your heart to your brain. I just wanted to do it, and Harold made it no better. Leading with his attitude, he was a hot-head, a take-no-shit kind of guy others knew not to play around with. He wasn't letting anybody hold or borrow nothing. He innately knew every new game and hustle the streets would try to run at him. If you hit him, he hit back harder. Along with his heavy dislike of new faces, he was also controlling. His particular way of doing things was the only way he wanted it, and he wouldn't have it any other way.

After three months of casual dating, I would inform Harold that I had a son. My son was a deal breaker in any relationship; so if he wasn't okay with it, then he could keep it moving to the next girl. To his credit, he seemed cool about it and things started to become more and more serious between us. Although he seemed to hide a darker side, he knew how to have fun and be serious when I needed him to be, which really attracted me.

That winter, we would introduce each other to one another's family during the holidays. Joining me for Thanksgiving at my parents, Harold would get along fine. My mom didn't ask many questions. Whether she didn't want to know or was naive, I will never really know, but as long as she didn't ask, I wasn't going to tell her. Never having that close of a relationship with my step-father at the time, I didn't think he cared too much who I dated, as long as I wasn't over there asking for money.

"Toni, as long as you've got a pussy, you should never be broke," I remember him telling me on a car ride to the store after I asked him if I could get some money for a few personal products.

There was no doubt about it. My mother and Emerson were hard workers and held steady jobs their whole lives, both retiring from Ford after thirty years of service. The street life wasn't anything they'd known, let alone condone—but as long as Harold made me happy, that was good enough for them. My brothers were indifferent; they liked him enough, it seemed. One by one, they welcomed him into the family, and we would all spend many nights together partying and having a great time.

As snow fell that Christmas Day, Harold pointed out the rundown liquor store, with its deteriorating façade, where he first started pushing dime bags. As we traveled through the East Side, he pointed out the field where he played football growing up, and other streets where he'd gotten into a shoot-out. Harold grew up in one of the roughest parts of Detroit's East Side, near the corner of Mack and Vick. It was obvious that his childhood was no picnic.

His mother, Patricia, opened the door that day, sweating from slaving away in the kitchen, and ushered us inside. She was warm, welcoming, and seemed to be sweet. Edith was cool and down to party, along with Gretchen, who had a black-sheep label cast upon her by the family. Even still, everyone got along just fine. Matt, the youngest brother out of the bunch, and Harold seemed to always have an unspoken rivalry, which festered for years. They would trade slight barbs, here and there, with a tone of utter disapproval. They were fundamentally different. Although Harold graduated high school, he didn't do much with his diploma after graduating. Matt, however, had great aspirations of joining the military and later going on to attend college. Nevertheless, the night seemed to go well. Harold exchanged gifts with his family, and I seemed to find common ground with Gretchen and Edith, leading us to spend many other girls' nights blacking out and throwing up out of car windows.

These tremendous highs were usually followed by devastating lows. Harold began to become more and more abusive, both verbally and physically, like a lethal combination of alcohol and prescription drugs. We pushed each other further into destruction.

In time, we would learn to push each other's buttons and do things that we knew would send the other into a rage. Jealousy and distrust would lead him to grow more aggressive. At first, like many women, I would be in denial about his behavior, brushing it off or blaming my own behavior.

"Harold? What's all that noise?" Patricia yelled just before I tumbled down a flight of stairs.

Harold had driven me all the way over to his house that night and I was ready to go home. This is when his dark side would rear its ugly head. What started as a back-and-forth debate quickly escalated into him turning red and going crazy, his face twisted and snarled—unlike anything I had ever seen before.

"I just want to go . . ."

Right before I could finish, he swung his fist and began shoving me out the door. Harold lived on a detached second floor, which could only be accessed by a steep flight of stairs around back in a dark alley of his family home. As he pushed me out the door while punching me, I tried to hold on, frightened I'd plummet down the staircase. The whole time, I was hoping his mother would do more or come running, but she must have been just as scared of him as I was. Her call was just enough to make him stop abruptly. I shot down the stairs and ran.

That was the first time Harold put his hands on me, but certainly not the last. I blamed myself. I thought, *Surely, it's my smart mouth and terrible attitude that set him off.* I would come to learn that it could be almost anything that would trigger him to snap and lose his cool. Cuts and bruises, from pulling out my hair to breaking my nose, would leave me in doubt about our relationship, unsure of how much more of it I could take. A nefarious cheater, too, Harold carried himself as a playboy. I would steadily grow unhappy and wished to break things off for good. Every incident would come with an apology and promises that it would never happen again, and I would foolishly believe it.

# REVOLVING DOOR

Finally, though, I'd had enough pain and suffering and I began to rebel. I started hanging out all hours of the night with my girls while meeting new guys. As is true about many men, Harold could dish out the misery, but could not take it. One late night, I came stumbling out of some corner bar on the West Side with Alphonso Woodward by my side—this was where Harold would catch us and totally lose it. Alphonso was a much older guy who had left the streets alone and opened and operated his own car wash, off the Southfield Freeway. He was handsome, with dark piercing eyes, soft locks of curly hair, and dark skin.

"Come on down, I'll wash your car for ya!" This was his pickup line to get me and many others.

This prompted Harold to rampage my apartment. I returned one evening to find the place ransacked and destroyed. Food had been scattered everywhere; dishes pulled from their cabinets; clothes cut, torn, and destroyed; holes left throughout the doors and walls. It left me devastated and struggling to salvage what I could, before apartment management deemed me a problematic tenant and kicked me out.

"You think he was mad?" Carol said sarcastically as she surveyed the damage. I shot back a look of disdain; then we both burst out in laughter.

"Can you believe his crazy ass?"

Feeling embarrassed, I would try to forget the incident and not share with anyone what had happened. I felt relief to be away from Harold's grip and on my own again. Whenever my mom would ask, I'd give her some bum excuse and quickly change the subject.

"Oh, he's been down South with family," I'd say. "Yeah, he's been really busy lately."

I played the role of the totally clueless girlfriend really well when friends inquired about his whereabouts or the circumstances of our breakup.

"Hey, where has Harold been?" Jazz would ask me.

"Who?" I'd retort back.

We'd burst out laughing by just sharing a look and she knew it was a signal I wanted to drop the subject. Harold was gone for good and just a part of my past. He had become unimportant—at least, that's what I would tell myself.

Jazz was a childhood friend of mine who grew up in the same neighborhood and knew a great deal about me. After Harold disappeared, I would soon fall back into hanging out on the block with her, drinking and doing drugs.

"Yeah, okay," she would say, unconvinced.

I'd ignore her and push thoughts of Harold to the back of my mind.

Eventually things would move more steadily with Alphonso, and we had started to date casually. He was from the West Side, like me, and quite popular with the street guys. Most of the girls would pull their cars into his car wash, hoping he'd come out to write them an order ticket. Even with all his charm, there always seemed to be something I couldn't quite put my finger on. He was naturally quiet and a private person, who kept to himself most of the time, but a niggling doubt about him would always stick in the back of my head.

It was the things that we did and the way he moved. We avoided most of the popular places, and he would relegate his calls to me at unusual times or full-on disappear for days. Even still, I trusted him and believed he was the one for me.

Since Alphonso was older, he had his shit together, and was much calmer and down-to-earth than the guys I had dated, up until that point. Later, I would learn that none of those qualities amount to much of anything, especially when the feeling isn't mutual. In the winter of 1985, I discovered I was pregnant with my second child. It was during February that I noticed I was late for my menstrual cycle.

"Girl, I'm late," I whispered into the receiver of the phone, as if someone besides Carol was listening on the other end.

*"Late?!"* Carol shrieked, sounding both confused and shocked.

"I think I'm pregnant."

"Pregnant? Pregnant by whom? Do you know who the daddy is?"

"Yeah, girl . . . Alphonso!"

Of course, I knew who the father was. At that point, I hadn't seen Harold in over a year, and Alphonso was the only other man I'd been sleeping with. Almost dumbfounded, I just didn't expect it, nor would I have wanted it to happen the way it did. Shit, even still, I hardly knew Alphonso. Just to be sure, I asked Carol to grab a pregnancy test kit before returning from the store.

With the pregnancy kit in hand, she frowned as she came through the doorway. I could tell Carol wasn't pleased I was possibly pregnant by Alphonso. She never trusted and hardly liked him from day one, always having the suspicion he was hiding something. She would have preferred I dated someone else more my speed and age. Regardless, she still had my back and supported whatever dumb situation I got myself in.

Squatting over the toilet, with all the trepidation in the world, I released onto the small device that would decide my fate. It seemed that the more anticipation I felt, the longer it took for the little white stick to give out a positive or negative reading. Dread filled my body at the thought of having to tell Alphonso that I was pregnant by him. I sat and imagined what his reaction would be, his steely demeanor and piercing eyes staring back at me, emotionless.

The reading finally came back, and just as I suspected, it was positive. Now I would have to tell him. Several days would go by as I pondered, worried, and wracked my brain about how best to approach Alphonso with the news. I was of two minds about it— hoping for a joyful reaction from him receiving the news well, and deep sadness this wouldn't be the type of news he wanted to hear. I realized I would eventually have to get it over with and tell him. Finally working up the nerve, I called him at the car wash and requested that we meet.

"Ah, well, I'm a little swamped today." As he tried to brush me off, as he often did, I refused to take no for an answer. It took all the courage in me to even call, let alone get up the nerve to break the news to him. I couldn't wait another day. If I did, I'd run the risk of losing the courage altogether and never tell him he was going to be a father.

"I know you're busy all the time, but this can't wait. Just meet me at Bert's."

He begrudgingly agreed to meet me that evening at the old jazz club in the Eastern Market, near downtown.

"I'm pregnant!" I cried out.

After only exchanging pleasantries, we hadn't even gotten nestled into our booth before I told my truth. The cat was out of the bag. Alphonso sat back in his seat, his eyes fixed on me without any sign of emotion. His silence was deafening.

*What a piece of shit!* I thought. Then I blurted out, "Well . . ."

"Well, what?" he shot back. "You're not keeping it, are you?" he asked before I could think how to respond.

Frozen in shock, I hadn't considered how callous his reaction would be. Suddenly filled with regret, I wasn't sure I should have told him—at least, not before considering if abortion was an option, which hadn't even crossed my mind.

"I want to, yeah!"

He bristled in his seat, as if calculating the best way to navigate this tricky situation and come out with an answer that would both satisfy and neutralize me into the decision that he preferred I make.

"I don't!" he blurted out, as if the right words eluded him. "I mean, I can't tell you *not* to keep it, but I don't want anything to do with it."

Maybe those were not the exact words he muttered as I began

to drift into a fog, but they seemed to be the gist of it. I sank farther down in my chair, dazed, as he went on rationalizing some tired excuse. The feelings of abandonment and loneliness I once felt as a child all came over me. It felt like I had swallowed a grapefruit at the thought that my unborn child would be fatherless, much like I was. As reality set in that I was going to be a single mother again, something in me snapped.

"Fine!" I went from a feeling of despair to anger. *This arrogant prick thinks we need him,* I thought. We as humans are built with the innate response of fight or flight. I chose to fight. I wouldn't need him or his help raising my child.

"I don't need you, and my baby—sure the hell—doesn't, either!" Attention from others would turn to us as I began to shout, rising from the table. "Me and mine gonna be good!" I stood above him with a look of death across my face as he remained seated quietly. I quickly grabbed my belongings and swiftly made an exit as the eyes in the place followed me out.

On September 19, 1985, I would welcome into the world my middle son, Jason. Without hesitation, I would leave the father's name blank on his birth certificate and set out as a single mother to raise both him and Marlon.

Even with Harold gone, the habits he left me stuck. We stayed up all hours of the night and day—drinking, partying, and doing drugs.

"Come on, just try it," Jazz would say as she urged me to try crack for the first time. Jazz and her boyfriend, Calvin, had actually been the pair who would introduce me to the addictive narcotic.

Sometime after moving back home, and Darry totaling my car, I'd call Jazz for a ride to work. I would never make it to work that day after Jazz explained she needed to run back to her house to grab something. It was like she set me up to get high. We ended up back at her place, where Calvin was already high and waiting.

"Come on, stop being scared. It ain't gonna hurt you!" Amused, Calvin would shove the pipe into my hand.

Once again, I would fall back in with my old crew. Jazz, Calvin, and Ms. Barbara, another girl from the neighborhood, and I would all meet up and get high. We sometimes would go into the park, where we knew there would be no interruptions, and go escape reality. We'd just get high and look up at the sky. Slowly I would begin to slip away, becoming more dependent on the drug. Day in and day out, it would become a necessity to perform even the simplest of tasks. I just couldn't stop.

As I became both mentally and physically addicted, even my appearance started to have a noticeable change. My skin and pores became dark and oily from the toxins. My eyes grew bags underneath them from lack of sleep and my body became frail from a poor diet. Those around me were increasingly concerned.

"Damn, Tonesa. Have you been eating?" Emerson asked me during one of my visits back home.

"Yeah, yeah, of course!" I replied.

It wasn't hard to tell I was lying, let alone high as a kite. I would come in speaking all fast and hyper, not letting anyone get a word in edgewise as I dropped Marlon and Jason off and was back out the door. It was things like this that made me realize I was headed down the wrong path. I had liberated myself from Harold, but the drugs were still there. The effort to try to wean myself off was ineffective. Just as I was telling myself I wasn't going to do any more, I would take one more hit, convincing myself every day that would be the last one. In my heart, I knew that wouldn't be the case.

Jazz and her habit had been the precursor to me realizing I needed to get clean. She had a habit of getting too high and overdosing. It seemed she could never get high enough. She would pack a pipe and take what appeared to be the biggest hits. Unable to stop her, I'd watch in fear as she'd take deep inhales until her eyes rolled to the back of her head, shoulders slumped over, and her mouth started to foam.

"Shit!" Calvin exclaimed the first time it occurred. He apparently was used to her and others getting too high. He picked her lifeless body up and rushed her into the bathroom, where he placed her in the tub, running cold water over her body until she regained consciousness.

It was only because of this time that I knew how to revive her during the subsequent times when she would do it with me, without him accompanying us. The third time, when it happened, her body shut down and it sent chills down my spine. Struggling, I pulled her from the living room into the bathroom and into the tub. In what felt like hours, it took several minutes for the cold water to work and bring Jazz back. I had no idea what I was going to do if she hadn't woken up.

In shock, I gathered my things and left without saying another word to her. It would be a while before I would see Jazz again after that incident. She would eventually get into some trouble; and with her mother unwilling to bail her out, she was sent to the county jail. Meanwhile, I fell asleep while getting high in a local park with Ms. Barbara one evening, and she stole $1,000 right from my purse. Having hustled all day for that money, only so I could continue to get high, I had finally had enough.

My mother had been urging me to enter a drug program. After several months of saying I was going and then changing my mind, I finally called and told her I was ready. It was a typical drug program, where you adhere to the rules of abstinence and participate in group meetings. These meetings were to help you get to the root of your addiction. The group counselor would educate us about drug addiction being caused by outside influences that pushed us to medicate to cope.

I knew I had a problem, but it damn sure didn't have anything to do with how my parents or boyfriend treated me. I just liked it too damn much was my problem. Even still, I would start to ponder if Emerson's treatment or my biological father's disappearance had any relation to my inclination to bend the rules. Regardless, I didn't give it much credence as the withdrawal symptoms left me drained and in physical pain. Fighting through cold sweats and bouts of nausea, I would push these thoughts away.

*I did this stuff because I wanted to,* I thought.

After the program was complete, I swore off drugs, or at least the heavy stuff. I promised myself I would stick to drinking alcohol and smoking a joint, every now and then. At least with those things, I didn't have to worry about the effects or being unable to control my addiction.

I had only been back at my mom's house for a little over a week when a brand-new gold Volvo came flying down the street. Harold emerged out of the car dressed head to toe in Gucci. Sure enough, he came to show out and to swoop me right back up into a relationship. Harold would quickly claim Jason as his own son, and the subject of Alphonso, or our relationship together, would never come up again. This was only after those two idiots would get into a shoot-out in the middle of the street with the baby in the car.

Never actually having seen Jason, except in a single photo my mother had given to him, Alphonso would never come around again.

# Chapter 5

# The Brothers

*Detroit, 1987*

IN MY ABSENCE, HAROLD HAD MADE INROADS TO BE THE PREMIER dealer on the East Side. He had built a team, a system, and would move kilos at a time. To survive in the streets and truly have longevity, you have to be smart, but also intuitive. It's not just numbers and weight, but having a sense of when someone is lying, setting you up, or not being who they say they are. It's not always easy spotting a fake person in a crowd or in the throes of a deal. Like with everything else, you have to rely on others to reach success and avoid the pitfalls that come with it.

Harold was an ace with numbers, and he didn't take shit from anyone. He lacked trust in virtually everyone; so when it came to second opinions, he relied on me heavily. He'd ask me what I thought of people he dealt with, how he should proceed on certain decisions, or how to deal with family issues. Even though he didn't always heed my advice, he believed there were times I could be more perceptive than he was.

It was a volatile situation that inspired both fear and excitement. It was easy to be pulled in by the trappings of the life. Harold taught me how to cut crack and bag it. I'd go and handle a deal occasionally, and we got to shop and buy anything we wanted. It just became increasingly harder to extricate myself from him and the streets. Harold would leave me with a permanent bruise on my nostril after I attempted once more to break things off. He'd drive over to Coyle Street to see my friends and me hanging out, sending him into another fit of rage.

"I just—don't wanna be together," I said hesitantly, right before Harold hauled off and struck me in the face.

Increasing fear made it hard for me to speak my mind or think it was possible to leave the relationship. Despite my hesitations, we would begin to build a life together. Moving in together in our own place, and vacationing as often as I could. Even still, I would wake up every morning, take the kids to school, then head to work, before I moonlighted as a drug dealer's girlfriend at night.

"I want you to meet these young dudes I'm thinking of working with. They're sharp," Harold mentioned after arriving home one day.

He had met two brothers from Southwest Detroit who were looking for a new plug and they approached him. "Sharp" meant they were smart, quick on their feet, and had potential. Still, it didn't make much sense to me at the time. Harold already had a pretty good system and a team of guys running the supply for him. Besides that, these boys didn't have much money to pay him. Regardless, he seemed excited for me to meet them and I obliged.

It was a nice summer day, and we all arranged to meet on Coyle Street. Darry and Ernest, along with Jazz and her family, plus some more of our friends around the neighborhood, gathered on the porch and lawn as we drank and played music and card games. Harold was already there, speaking to Darry, when I drove down the street in the brand-new Corvette he had just bought me.

# THE BROTHERS

"Ay, there go Toni! Damn!" Jazz and some of our friends would yell out as they noticed me pull up.

As I got out, I noticed what appeared to be a gold Buick in the driveway. Four young guys sat there looking at me as I made my way toward Harold.

"Is that them?" I asked him.

"Yeah, let me introduce you." Harold motioned for the brothers to get up and walk toward their parked car. "This is Demetrius. This is my wife, Toni."

"What's goin' on?" Demetrius held out his hand for me to shake. He was light-skinned, skinny, and talked with a deep drawl.

"And this is his brother, Terry."

"Hey, how you doin'?" He reached out his hand toward me, with a big smile across his face.

Despite both of them looking like young boys, they were total opposites. In contrast to Demetrius's fair skin, Terry was brown-skinned, his eyes were bright, and his demeanor seemed more charming and cheerful. He looked deep into my eyes and seemed to pause.

"Nice meeting you two!" Keeping it short, I smiled and headed toward the house.

"Come on, what we drinking?" I yelled to Jazz and the girls, leaving Harold to talk with the boys.

That day, moving forward, Harold would begin to work with the brothers. He assigned them small jobs, here and there, and rewarded them with work to sell on their own. They could also come to him to put a play together if they said they had a buyer and needed more supply than they could afford. Harold would front them the work, and they'd return with his cut of the proceeds. He built a rapport with the brothers and began hanging out, gambling, and drinking with them, and even inviting them over to the house for dinner.

This relationship would work for a while. But then, Harold deduced, "Man, he a fool!" That's how he summed up Terry's older brother Demetrius's character.

"He said he wants to go out like Scarface!" remarked Harold.

That, along with a few other comments, made Harold uneasy and unsure if he wanted to continue doing business with the unpredictable older sibling. Then after a night at the gambling house observing Demetrius lose all the money he owed to Harold and others, Harold decided to sever all ties with him. (Truthfully, I'm not even certain if Demetrius ever repaid Harold.)

After this, Terry made it his job to make up for his brother's failures. He seemed to make a concerted effort to make his way around Harold and me, when he could, making himself as useful as possible. Harold didn't mind much, as he could see that Terry had potential and a good head on his shoulders. He paid his debts, got the job done, and had a good reputation. At the time, I didn't think much of him other than he was a sweet young guy who always spoke and helped out.

In time, Terry would begin to reveal that his interest in sticking around wasn't strictly financial. He had taken a keen interest in getting to know me, despite the fact I was the boss's soon-to-be wife. In contrast, I had little interest, even as friends.

I feared what Harold would do if he had any suspicion. Leaving the refrigerator dusty could cause him to fly off the handle, let alone the idea of me striking up an interest in a young man who worked for him.

The danger did not stop Terry from trying. He would begin popping up at the house, unannounced, with one excuse or another.

"Hey, I'm trying to reach Harold," he'd say, or, "Hey, H told me I could come pick that up from you."

Whatever it was, he'd find a way to get over to the house and linger a little longer than needed. It would all come to a head when he began showing up at my place of work. Terry showed up one day at the travel agency, without any warning, to purchase tickets to St. Louis, and there I was with two black eyes. A total mess I tried to cover up with makeup and eye shadow, but even Stevie Wonder would have been able to see those bruises.

Horrified, Terry came around my desk and caressed my face.

"Who did this to you?"

I began to weep quietly. I could see in his eyes when he realized that I was a victim of domestic abuse at the hands of Harold.

"I'm gonna make a bunch of money and take you away from this," Terry whispered as he wiped my tears away. Without saying another word, Terry left and it became our secret.

Occasionally, he'd come by and take me to lunch, and we'd talk about everything—life, our ambitions, love, cars, clothes, and whatever else we could think of. He became a friend to me, when I desperately needed one.

Despite it all, even my brother Darry couldn't save me, because I *didn't want* to be saved. In some twisted logic, I thought it was what I deserved. I also thought what I could get out of it was worth it. I enjoyed the risks and the adventures that came with it. I don't know where I got it from, but a lot of things seemed to come naturally to me. I could think quickly on my feet or get us out of a tight jam in a heartbeat.

"That a real Rolex?" an undercover cop asked after pulling me and Harold over for questioning.

"It's fake! You think I got that type of money!" I quipped back.

Meanwhile, the police had separated us, and Harold popped off, "Fuck you! Of course, my watch is real!"

We had been followed, but fortunately were not caught with anything. They had no credible evidence against us, so we were both released—and not without them returning *my* Rolex. It was real, of course, but I wouldn't tell no federal agent that.

Harold either just didn't think that way or let his emotions get the best of him. They kept his, citing he needed to provide receipts of purchase, which would have been a fool's errand.

It wouldn't be the first or last time my quick wit would be several steps ahead of him.

# Chapter 6

# Bus Ride

*1988 to 1992*

FRED MADE A RIGHT ONTO MICHIGAN AVENUE AND HEADED NORTH, back toward our hotel. Fred was Harold's plug, who had a direct connection to the Colombians down in Texas. I'm not exactly sure where Fred was from or how the two met, but he was well-liked around the city. When we came into Chicago, he'd chauffeur us around to pick up several kilos and show us a good time before we headed back to Detroit.

"I'll take y'all down to this spot on the West Side. Man, they got the best drinks," he boasted before his eyes darted to the rearview mirror.

"What's up?" Harold asked.

Squinting some more, Fred had taken notice of something. "I think we're being followed."

He made a quick left onto a smaller street. Careful not to change speeds or make it obvious we had taken notice of the same car following not too far behind, Fred became visibly nervous.

"Shit, man, shit!"

"Just be cool, man. Just be cool," Harold responded.

"Y'all gone have to get out, fuck!"

Harold looked around, alarmed. "Get out where?"

"Here." Fred made another turn and then brought the car to a stop. "Get out. I'll try to lose them. Take your bags!"

Just like that, Fred put Harold and me out on some random street corner in the inner city of Chicago's South Side. Carrying two bags, with sixty kilos apiece, and dressed to the nines, we stuck out like sore thumbs.

"What the hell we gone do?" Harold was visibly upset and panicked. Neither one of us knew the city that well, or where the hell we even were.

"Shit, man. We got all this shit on us. He's trying to get us killed!" I examined the street, looking both up and down the boulevard. "We'll just get on the bus." Just then, I noticed a city bus sign a few feet in front of us.

"What?" Harold responded.

"Come on, we'll just have to take the bus somewhere safer."

Harold was apprehensive and looked at me with disbelief in his eyes. It was the best option we had, and damn sure better than sitting on some sidewalk, in a city we hardly knew, carrying several kilos of cocaine with us. Not to mention we were both dressed in designer clothing and accessories—him in gator lace-ups, his gold chain, and both of us wearing Rolexes, with diamond bezels. Taking the bus was better than being sitting ducks waiting for someone to rob us, or the police showing up to inquire about the black duffels we were carrying.

The bus finally pulled up and we climbed on board. Harold pulled out his bankroll of money and slipped some singles into the machine before the driver closed the doors and took off. All eyes were on us as we headed toward the back, past all the other riders. We certainly didn't fit in with the rest of the people and I tried my best not to make it obvious. Harold, though, couldn't keep himself together. He was nervous as we took our seats near the back, gazing out the window, sweat forming on his forehead. He tried his best to hide his uneasiness, looking toward the ceiling of the bus.

"We can just ride this until we get somewhere better and call a cab," I mentioned.

Harold and I arrived back at our car, loaded up, and then hightailed it back to Detroit that night, without running into any more issues. I'd go along for the ride several more times that year before discovering I was pregnant with my third child.

Harold was beyond elated to learn I was having another boy—his first son. Although I was ecstatic, I realized that this only pushed me down a road I was unsure of. Now, even if I found the courage, I couldn't just leave; and with a child on the way, we would undoubtedly be a part of each other's lives forever.

The following summer, at almost two weeks past my due date, I would go into labor the day of my birthday.

"What kind of name is Corey!" Emerson shrieked in his Southern accent.

"It's the name I'm giving him. I like it," I responded.

"Now you know you need to name that boy after his father," Emerson said calmly.

Deep down, I knew he was right. Most fathers wanted to have a son named after themselves, and Harold was no different. Despite this, I wasn't too fond of the name Harold, nor was I too excited to be naming my son after him. I listened to my stepfather and reluctantly changed his first name to Harold, making Corey his middle name.

The good times rolled on. Harold would continue to make large sums of money and take trips. We'd fly to Vegas for a Mike Tyson fight or to Florida to catch a cruise through the Gulf. We'd hit Chicago and party with Fred when we could. Harold had plans to get out of the game at thirty-five, and he was well on his way—until things began to take a drastic turn.

I had just put dinner on the table one evening when Harold got the call that Fred had been killed. Things looked bleak now, with his plug gone. Harold would have to scramble to find someone else he could trust to pick up from. A week later, we flew down to Chicago to attend the funeral and pay our respects.

"Thank y'all for coming." Linda, Fred's wife, came up and gave me and Harold a warm hug. An already-skinny woman, she looked quite frail. Her makeup was smeared from the tears that ran down her bony cheeks. Wearing a black dress covered in fringe, she tried to hide her face behind a veil.

"Fred really loved you two, he always spoke so highly."

"He was a good dude." Harold's eyes looked down toward the ground, clearly unable to look Linda in her face. It was a rough loss for both of them. Death is a guaranteed part of the game, but it never gets any easier, especially for someone as well-liked as Fred was.

"There's someone here who wants to meet you." She wrapped her arm around Harold's and pulled him away just as the mood in the room began to change. Someone turned on the jukebox and drinks started being served. We spent the rest of the evening drinking and getting to know some of Fred's closest friends and family, including George.

"Fred told me a lot about you," he said.

George was Colombian and had a link with the cartel through Texas and apparently Fred's connection. He made it a point not only to come lay Fred to rest, but to connect with some of the people Fred did business with. Now that Fred was gone, the Colombians would have to find someone else to use as a channel to supply their drugs to the inner cities. Fred obviously spoke highly of Harold and how much he was picking up at a time, and this impressed them enough to seek him out when the time came.

Harold left giddier and more excited than somebody should after leaving a funeral.

"You know what this means?" he asked.

Now that Fred wouldn't be middlemanning the deal anymore, the price Harold would pay would go down. It could only mean he would make more money and have less of a hassle getting the product he wanted. I stayed silent and let him gloat on the way back to our room. He wouldn't be singing their praises for too long.

We touched down in Houston, Texas, in the spring of 1990 and prepared to meet with George's contacts. We checked into our room and Harold went to arrange a meetup. "Yeah, yeah, I seen it on the way to our hotel," he said through the phone.

I don't know why, but things felt strange to me from the beginning. We headed out to our rental car and drove to the meeting spot. Harold pulled the car into another hotel driveway and valeted the car. I can't remember the name of the place, but it put me in mind of a Ritz or Westin. It was posh, and the clientele you could tell were upper-class customers, and mostly white. The lobby smelled of fresh flowers and buzzed with life, and the bar was somewhat crowded with patrons. There, George, joined by another gentleman, waved us down.

"My friends, what's up?"

"How you doin?" Harold responded as he shook their hands.

"How was your trip? This is my associate Danny."

Danny nodded and we all took a seat.

"Should we order drinks?" George asked. He was warm, but something seemed off. While we agreed to have a drink, I sat quietly. They would exchange pleasantries about the trip and missing Fred before getting into discussing business. Things continued to seem off. I couldn't put my finger on it, but something in my gut said that it was a setup.

It was then that I noticed two men over at the next table from us. A red flag waved in my head. They didn't seem to fit in with the rest of the crowd. Although they were white, they didn't dress like the rest of the clientele or appear to be drinking. I stayed quiet while Harold talked terms and numbers with George and his friend. Suddenly he nudged me under the table and looked to me for reassurance, but I remained silent, not speaking a word. When it was over, Harold shook their hands with a grin and we departed.

"Why wasn't you saying nothing?" Harold asked, annoyed.

"I think they're the cops!"

"The cops? Those were Fred's dudes!" he exclaimed.

Despite this, Harold worked the deal out with them, and they arranged to have him pick it up, and we returned to Detroit. We were back home and I urged and begged him not to call.

"Please don't call, babe! It doesn't feel right. Fuck them! Don't call, I'm telling you it isn't right."

As much as I tried to convince him, Harold wasn't sure it was the right idea. He didn't want them to think he had run off with their money or drugs, but he begrudgingly agreed. Despite agreeing, he walked around the house agitated and on edge most of that day. He paced, chewed the inside of his cheek, and shifted back and forth in his seat.

"I'm gonna make a few runs," he said, leaping up.

Against my warnings, Harold left the house, found a pay phone, and called down to Texas. The Colombians kept him on the phone long enough that federal agents were able to pinpoint his location and send a car to follow him that day. Every location he stopped at that day, they documented and eventually raided and were able to find stash spots of drugs and money. It would be his fingerprint on one of the bricks of cocaine that would secure an indictment.

# BUS RIDE

\* \* \*

"You told me, and I didn't listen."

Unfortunately, it was too late. He was now out on bail awaiting trial. Harold would have to begin putting his affairs in order to prepare for turning himself in to serve his sentence. He would sell off most of his cars, store his jewelry, and stash whatever money he could collect off the streets. His attorney would even advise us that it was best to get married, as a matter of appearance to the judge on the case.

I didn't want to get married at all, but I agreed. It could have been fear I felt: fear of what he would do, fear of what it could mean for me and my own freedom. His lawyer thought it was best at the time in case they tried to indict me as well. It would protect us, since a wife can't be compelled to testify against her husband.

As I walked down the aisle in my hot-pink wedding dress, I put on a fake smile for all our friends and family. Everyone looked on in joy as I sank further into my own dark world of regret. It didn't feel like the right thing to do, but what choice did I have? Besides, I still loved Harold and wanted to help him. If I could do anything to help his case, I would, and I'd stand by him until he finished his sentence.

Almost two years later, Harold would cop a plea and be sentenced to a minimum of seven years in prison. He'd leave me to deal with a few of the guys he dealt with on the streets, including Terry, asking him to help me and look after me just in case anything went wrong. He said he would advise me as much as he could from behind bars.

# Chapter 7

# Helpless

*Victorville, California, 2010*

I T WAS EARLY IN THE MORNING, JUST BEFORE DAWN, WHEN WE AWOKE to the sound of muffled sobs from Anita. Anita was a young mother who fell victim to a man who didn't care what happened to her. He had orchestrated drug runs, using her as a mule, until the Feds caught up to him. He bargained for his own freedom by implicating her as the mastermind. Now, as she lay on her cot, she would spend many sleepless nights wondering where her children were.

"Babe, what's wrong?" I asked.

"I don't know where they are!" she cried out in desperation. "My kids," she continued. "I don't know where they are!"

I jumped from my prison bunk bed and tried to console Anita. I cradled her against my chest and ever so gently rubbed her back. While comforting her, I imagined the horrifying feeling of not knowing where my children were.

"It's okay, it's okay," I attempted to say soothingly, trying to reassure her that everything would be fine.

"They're somewhere waiting on their momma. I'm sure they wouldn't want you so worried," I said while lifting her face and gently holding it in my hands.

"You gonna make your time here especially hard by worrying too much."

Anita just kept on weeping quietly.

"You just focus on getting yourself together and getting home."

I couldn't believe it myself. I wasn't even sure I believed what I heard coming out of my own mouth. My heart ached and pained with guilt just knowing I was placed in such a situation. It had to be a gut-wrenching struggle every day to get up and be talked down to by the guards and counselors, live with multiple personalities, be locked far away from your family, and not know how they were doing, especially young boys and girls.

Anita wasn't the only one with a story like that. Many of the women struggled to see their families because of unstable situations or merely their parents being too old to travel up and down the long highways. For the most part, we were each other's family—at least while we traveled this same journey.

"Guess what today is?" I asked with a smirk.

Anita laughed as she sniffled and wiped her nose. "Friday!" she responded.

"That's right, and I got something special for us tonight. So get some sleep."

Just like spending the week getting up, heading out to work, and handling whatever mundane task lay on the agenda, feverishly waiting on the weekend, it was the same in prison. It was usually more relaxed around camp, as most of the counselors and higher-ups were off, while the weekend staff was more lenient regarding patrolling and disciplinary actions. It was when we ladies would gather around, let our hair down, and party—or whatever you could attempt to call it in an all-women gathering

with contraband smuggled from the kitchen, through visita-
tions, government-issued jukeboxes. And if you couldn't afford or
have the ability to get liquor from the outside, there was home-
made moonshine.

The ladies and I planned to turn up this weekend and I had a
nice bottle of Patrón tucked away just for the occasion. Anita and I
would be drinking away our worries tonight and counting down
another day until freedom. Through my time at Victorville Women's
Facility, I met a lot of extraordinary women with compelling
stories—tales that most people wouldn't believe or could even
conceive. It is easy to get caught up in the notion of what you
would do in certain situations or color experiences in our own as-
sumptions and misconceive who people are. It is through strife
and shared times like this that life and God will debunk those mis-
conceptions and alter our perspective. Sharing stories, we discovered we were all more alike than different. Most of us shared the
same fears, worries, and hopes contained within similar stories of
love, loss, betrayal, and family, which resonated in all of us.

"Girl, I did everything," lamented Valerie, shrugging her
shoulders with a certain layer of lethargy blanketing an "it is what
it is" attitude.

"I cooked it, packaged it, shit . . . sold most of it. Not including
feeding him and fuckin' him!" she went on to say. "Next thing I
know, my door is being blown off the hinges and the Feds are
rushing through it."

She stopped and grabbed her cup of tequila before taking a
swig to drink down the taste of the past. You could see the sparkle
of regret as she looked off at the linoleum floors, before bursting
back into the story with excitement. "Next thing I know, he's
jumping out of bed butt-ass naked, hollering, 'Take her!'" She
burst out laughing. "'It was all her. That's all her shit and I'm
over here with no clothes on, confused and shit.'"

Our hearty laughs came from a place of understanding. The

irony of loving and wanting to protect someone, who would actually sell each one of us out in a heartbeat, is a pathetic commonality in an otherwise-extraordinary group of women.

Debbie, on the other hand, a fifty-something ex-prostitute and mother, steered the conversation toward sex. She liked to compete with the younger women, hopping up that evening and pulling out her tits.

"Come on, show me yours! Whose look better?" she bantered to Amish.

Amish was only twenty-six and never had children, and it was clear who would win the contest, but Debbie needed a clear view of the rack Amish was blessed with, displayed outside her pale blue button-up.

We were all there together: drug dealers, smugglers, prostitutes, fraudsters, meth and heroin addicts alike. We were all assigned to one pod, no matter our backgrounds or crimes, forced to find the similarities we shared rather than the differences. From crying in each other's arms about another woman answering our prison calls while away, to laughing about Debbie's exploits of being paid to piss on sex-deprived men. No one was better than the other, and the weekends lent a chance for us to let our hair down and show how rowdy we could get.

While there were many reprieves from the mundane and restrictive life in prison, other days could be unbearable. One good guard meant there were five other ones and a counselor you had to avoid at all costs, unless you wanted to make your time hard. Talking back or any kind of disorderly conduct meant time in the SHU (special housing unit), which was another word for "hole," no phone or visitation privileges—or worst of all, good time taken away. "Good time taken away" meant lengthening your sentence and tacking on more time, which could drive a person insane. I was especially scared when Counselor Mary Golsom threatened to take away my phone for back talk.

Golsom was a particular bitch from hell, with dirty-blond hair and a pasty-white face that reminded me of an elementary school teacher who sent you to a corner for acting up in class. At the mere utterance of her reprisal, you could lose your phone privileges. It was best to let her or anyone of similar stature hurl insults and question your existence than allow them to prod you into a rage, which could result in disciplinary action—not worth losing more time away from your children. It was the only thing that kept me together, knowing I had them to come home to.

"You're not like the rest of the girls," Aoki said in a deep Asian accent while looking down at her crossword. "Where you from?"

"Michigan. What about you?"

"Taiwan."

It wasn't normal for ladies to hang out or speak to others beyond their race, especially not Asians. They seemed to strictly get along among themselves, but I apparently didn't have a problem getting along with mostly everyone, regardless of their backgrounds.

"You shouldn't be here," she said with a smile, looking up at me. Her hair was perfectly coiled into locks that framed her pretty and vivacious round face. She was older, like me, but didn't seem like it. Her face was youthful and her outlook optimistic. After group meetings at the chapel, while most women would scatter back out the door, she would hang out and we would get to learn more about each other and one another's cultures.

"What you in for?"

"Ah, tax evasion," she replied. "A bunch of other SEC violations—insider trading," she continued. "You know the usual stuff." She shrugged and we both laughed. "So, you have two boys? I seen them on the visit."

"I have three, actually. My oldest is doing time as well. He's on my case."

"Oh," she replied, unsure of what to say. "I have two myself," she continued. "We never stop worrying, do we?"

"No, never," I responded, exasperated.

"Married?"

"No, divorced. What about you?"

"Thirty-seven years, he died." She looked on ahead, as if seeing the past. "A year ago. Cancer. Now it's just me and the boys." She smiled wistfully.

"I'm sure it's hard without him," I said.

"Eh," she grunted with a shrug and quizzical look on her face. "He didn't do much." She leaned into her chair as she gazed into space before bursting into a chuckle. "Don't get me wrong. He did good with the kids . . . and taking care of me. But breadwinner he was not. Couldn't make a dollar if he tried. I just didn't understand it, but . . . I loved him. He was there for me. He didn't mind me being the boss, but he was jealous. Not of the money, but of the attention."

She looked dead into my eyes with piercing directness. "You know what I mean? The long hours, coupled with the fact other men coveted me, if not for my looks, but for what I could do for them. Money, you know. It brought all these people around this love—and not one of them was there for me except my husband. We'd fight endlessly. 'You think these people care?' he'd ask, and I'd ignore him, and drink, only concerned with what these people could give me. Money . . . information."

She looked down into her lap with a look of shame. "It just about tore us apart and the boys had to see." She grimaced, wiping her face. "I let everything else make me forget what was important. I spent so much time blaming everyone else, but it was *me*. I killed my husband. My greed and selfishness tore us apart, and when he needed me most, I was in here." Tears streamed from her eyes.

Pangs of guilt would rush over all of us, ebbing and flowing. Some days were better than others, and the weight of it was specific to each woman. Aoki was a kind woman, but unlike most women serving time, she wasn't a victim of a man—rather the man was a victim of hers. She wrestled with the guilt of leaving her boys out on the street, much like me, but she fought with a deep guilt that she was the reason her husband had grown sick and had succumbed to cancer.

# Chapter 8
# Who Am I?

*1993 to 1995*

I HAVE NO IDEA WHO I THOUGHT I WAS, OR WHY I BELIEVED MY NEW-found freedom came with living life even more dangerously on the edge. I went where I wanted, did what I pleased, and dated whoever caught my eye. I ran my own operation under a veil of secrecy that only a handful of people knew about—and still maintained a nine-to-five while caring for my three boys.

Harold, now upstate serving his twenty-year sentence, didn't stop me or scare me away from the streets. Not having him around only drove me more. I had to fend for myself and continue to provide a lifestyle that I had grown accustomed to, let alone provide for my family, who had come to rely on me when they needed to make ends meet, or my friends like Terry, who entrusted me to make connections and orchestrate deals.

My total disregard for the law or the consequences of my actions would bleed over into my dating life as well when I met Clyde. He was a handsome gentleman with a cool down-to-earth demeanor and happened to work the gang unit of the Detroit Police Department. On occasion, he'd take private security jobs for celebrities who would visit town, which often led to a detail that would send him out of state or even the country. That was how we met, when he came strolling one evening into my job at the travel agency.

"Hi, welcome to Triple A. Is there something I can help you with?"

"Yeah . . . I am interested in, uh, booking a flight."

"Okay, I certainly can help with that. What's your destination?"

"Aruba," he responded.

"Aruba? Nice! Going on a vacation with a special someone?"

"No, I wish. Work, actually."

I began to type away at my workstation, looking at flight itineraries and pricing for his preferred dates, while we struck up a conversation about a myriad of things that would eventually lead to him inviting me.

"You should come down; it will be fun. I'm working a festival, maybe bring some friends and we can all hang out."

"Maybe," I said, blushing.

We exchanged contact information and soon after I called Carol to convince her to fly down with me.

We'd jet down to Aruba for the music fest and party with some of the hottest acts of the time: Boyz II Men, Gerald Levert, and even Chaka Khan. Watching them perform from backstage, then partying all over the island afterward until the wee hours of the morning, really appealed to us.

Clyde and I hit it off and continued to hang out, once we arrived back in town. He even got to know my boys and we'd all go on bike rides. He also took them to some events, like the auto show, or to see Sinbad do stand-up comedy, where Corey got to meet one of his favorite actors after the show.

Although I was fond of Clyde, my heart was still swayed toward the streets. The secrets I kept would loom over the entire relationship even as he sat at my kitchen table having no clue that just downstairs in my basement, I'd be storing a ton of "keys" for a friend.

"Hey, thanks for meeting me. I wouldn't usually bother you this late, but you're the only one I can trust," Nate said anxiously.

"Of course! You know I'll always be here for you. What's goin' on?"

Nate was a good friend of mine I had met dealing in the streets. It was one of those rare platonic relationships where we could have a good time, talk about our relationships, and call on each other in times of need. We trusted each other explicitly.

"The Feds picked me up. They were asking all types of questions, and I think they may still be following me."

"Oh, my God! So, like, what's going to happen? What do you need me to do?"

Nate shuffled through a coat pocket and pulled out a set of keys. "These are keys to my house in Southfield." He thumbed through them before stopping at a single gold key. "You'll need this one to get in."

"Okay?"

"There's two black duffels. I need you to get them."

"All right, all right."

"It's work in them. So you got to be extra careful, keep your eyes open," Nate said.

I can't explain how nervous I felt. It was like the small hairs on the back of my neck stood straight up. My heart was pounding, and my hands were sweaty. I picked up my brother Darry along the way to help me, as I didn't think I'd be able to do it alone.

"What's goin' on, sis?"

"I need your help. Come on, get in the car!"

Darry hopped in, without hesitation, without saying another word, and we headed down the highway toward Nate's house.

After we retrieved the two black duffel bags, we parked around back, a block over from my house. Then Darry helped me pack the cocaine into the ceiling of my basement and the back of a wall. Nate disappeared for a while and the kilos of cocaine stayed stored in my basement for months.

All this time, I conducted everyday life as if I didn't have a million dollars' worth of work, or a twenty-to-life prison sentence, just below my kitchen table. I went on with my normal routine of feeding the kids breakfast, helping them with homework, hosting friends and family, and conducting my own business right there without batting an eyelash.

Terry and his crew of friends would also roll through on random weeknights when I had work or just the kids. Demetrius, Shawn, "Pig," and a few others would come along to drink and party all night and just have a good time. Listening to music, talking about life, and cracking jokes on one another as the drinks began to kick in—over time we grew closer, and formed a "family" bond.

Times wouldn't be without their ups and downs for Terry, though. He and Demetrius would get into a beef with some dudes down in the southwest part of town, which led to a shoot-out resulting in him losing sight in his left eye after a botched surgery. Money was tight as well. Although Terry was compensated nicely from a lawsuit, the money he won against the hospital dried up fast. Besides buying a brand-new Range Rover, not much else came from it as he spent freely and took care of all the people around him. It was just like he could never get a firm footing and take off, like he seemed to have the potential to do. From the outside looking in, it appeared to be all good, but I stayed up with him many nights as he vented and griped about his financial issues.

"It's . . . my mom, my brother, everybody! You know?" Terry sighed as he lamented about an argument he'd just had with his mother. "I have been taking care of them for as long as I can remember—without even as much as a thank-you."

"Yeah, I know, but things will work out."

He shrugged off my encouragement, as if he wasn't so sure anymore.

"I bet it'd be pretty easy to make a million dollars," I quipped as I flipped chicken in a pan of hot grease. Just like many times before, a sinister idea played out in my head, and I began to indulge one more fantasy on a whim. "Me and you, I bet we could make a million dollars!"

Terry let out a hearty chuckle. "Yeah, all right!"

You could tell he wanted to believe it badly. His eyes glimmered with hope. I'm sure a fantasy in his head of just counting it played out at the back of his mind, but his head shook no. "What's this?"

As I put a plate of fried chicken, Rice-A-Roni, and spinach in front of him, I responded, "Spinach! You need to have a vegetable. All you dudes want to do is eat starches."

He looked at me with a childlike gaze and a smirk on his face.

"All you dudes act like something green gone kill you, and I tell you what, it's gone be all them starches and fried foods that kill you first."

"You right!" he replied.

"I *know*! I also know we gone make a million dollars. So you got to eat healthy."

Speechless, Terry laughed and dug into his plate without saying another word.

I would retire to bed that evening with ideas swirling in my head. I guess in so many ways that was the night everything changed. I would be the catalyst that changed the trajectory of not only our lives, but everyone's around us. I would awake the next morning with my own plan of how to get us started.

I picked up the phone and dialed the one person I knew I could call on to help.

"Hey, what up, Toni?" Nate's voice came across the other end of the receiver.

"Hey, Nate, I was wondering if I could talk to you about something."

"Sure, anything. Come by the crib."

I headed over to Nate's that night, determined to get him to agree to give Terry the leg up he needed. *The worst he could say is no,* I thought.

*BOOM!* The duffel bag landed next to Terry's feet with a thud.

"What's this?" Terry asked, perplexed.

"Open it!" Grinning, I gestured for him to unzip the bag.

Terry unzipped the bag and found the key to his empire. His eyes lit up with astonishment.

"Where . . . ?"

"You got ninety days to pay me back in full, and after that, you're on your own."

"Whatchu mean? We doin' this together," he replied. He looked up at me like he never had before, and it was like I felt his soul and could see his past, present, and future.

Pausing, we both leaned in. As my heart began to race, he kissed my lips.

# Chapter 9

# Shit Happens

*1995 to 1999*

"**N**INETY-EIGHT, NINETY-NINE . . . TEN."

"I got another ten here." Sitting with a pile of cash still at our feet, Terry handed me another wad of $100 bills held together by a single rubber band, which I placed with the rest of the counted money on my kitchen table.

"That's . . . Well, this already a million!" Astonished, I looked up at Terry, who was grinning.

"Watch, I'm gone get me a million and do whatever the hell I want," Demetrius, or "Meech," as he would come to be known, interjected.

"I can't believe you fucking did it, you did it!" Ignoring Meech's commentary, Terry and I embraced each other as I squeezed his cheek and smooched all over his face.

"It ain't just y'all that's about to get this money. I'm gone have it all!" Meech insisted.

Terry and Meech were very close brothers, but an underlying sibling rivalry seemed to simmer just below the surface. It would come out in random conversations and situations, and it gave me pause. Terry laughed it off most of the time. Chuckling, he said, "Yeah, bro, we in this together."

There's nothing like counting that first million and dreaming of all the possibilities. Chills went through my entire body, and I felt a euphoria I never experienced before. I felt accomplished, validated, and elated at the direction our lives had begun to take. I was beginning to fall for a man who had been a genuine friend, confidant, and partner.

The larger supply would necessitate a larger clientele and footprint. Terry was enterprising and sociable. He was liked a lot in his social group and made connections easily, which would only result in spreading outside the city and eventually the state. Chicago, St. Louis, Miami, New York, and Atlanta—followed by California— would all become prime markets. Terry would discover that for the same product that guys were buying back home, states like Missouri would pay triple the price, if not more.

Things were finally working out and Terry was well on his feet. As for me, it was all work-life balance. Waking up early mornings, fighting with the boys to get ready for school, cooking breakfast, packing lunches, ushering the boys out the door, and heading off to work. The evenings were spent running errands or taking care of some illicit agenda, then heading home to prepare dinner, get the kids ready for bed, entertaining Terry and the boys, and enjoying a nightcap with Clyde. Weekdays were chock-full of to-do lists, while the weekends allowed us more free time, as Corey spent most weekends with his grandmother, or I'd get the boys dressed and we'd head down the highway to visit Harold upstate.

Harold would glean what he could from our short visits and limited collect calls from prison about how things were going in the streets and with the kids. Still, he was left with a limited view of what was going on—namely, my changing feelings and growing strength to leave. In the years he remained in prison, my heart dreamed of a life where I didn't fear the man I was with, or that it would truly be love that surrounded me. Terry began to make me believe that I could have love and everything I dreamed of. For the most part, things ran smoothly and life seemed peaceful.

This peace wouldn't last long, though.

Harold was released from prison in the spring of 1999. Although I had expressed my desire for freedom and a divorce, before he was due to arrive, it wasn't easy to convey or convince him that I was serious, especially while on a prison call or during the short time in the visitors' room, where heavy subjects seemed to be avoided, as not to ruin the short time families had to see their loved ones.

Adjusting back to the streets wouldn't be easy for Harold or for me. He was disgruntled by his new fallen place in the hierarchy of the streets. He came home to the funds he had left behind being lower than he expected or remembered—something I'd undoubtedly take the blame for, even though he wouldn't leave it with me to safeguard.

I'd have conflicts about how best to handle the situation or get the message through that I wanted to move on with my life without him as a husband. Attempting to be friends, helping him find footing in a new world, and co-parenting only confused things and made it more difficult to sever the ties. Doubly difficult was the fact I decided to move on with a man who used to work for him and who was, more or less, a child when Harold left. Now that child was an adult male and growing ever more successful by the day.

I can't pretend to know or understand how Harold felt at the time. One thing is for sure: His world had changed and everyone in it was not who they were when he left. He had to grapple with the fact he wasn't the boss anymore—on top of me having one foot out the door, heading straight for another man.

\* \* \*

"Wow, this is your car?" Corey exclaimed as he ran toward Terry's new Mercedes-Benz CL500.

"Yeah, I paid a little extra to get it six months early," he boasted.

"Wow," I remarked.

"That muthafucka clean," Harold responded.

"Dad, why can't you get a car like this?" Corey asked.

Harold didn't respond as he looked on as Terry let Corey in to get a closer look at the inside of his brand-new ride.

I felt an uneasiness in my stomach as I imagined how Harold felt as his only son admired another man's accomplishment and questioned his own father's abilities. Resentment would grow, not only as Terry took his place as a husband, but as a father, too. Harold could concede his throne to the streets, but his family was one thing he wasn't willing to part ways with.

I feel I tried my best to make it work: to be there for Harold, to support and to help him get situated back into society. It would only go so far. Experience from the past, and fear he would revert to his old physically abusive ways, made me avoid bringing the topic of divorce into the conversation. Although Harold moved into his own place, rather than with the boys and me, I believe he had no doubts we would eventually rekindle our relationship. I'm not exactly sure when it clicked that this wouldn't be the case, but he would soon prove he wasn't willing to let me go so easily.

Meanwhile, on the other side of the country, Meech had put down roots in California. This state was a hot spot for lower prices, thanks to its proximity to the Mexican border, where the majority share of drugs flowed into the United States. To gain connections and cut out as many middlemen as possible, the brothers had to go to the West.

Meech initially made headway, securing connections and running into the right people. While there, he met Wayne, an older gentleman who ran a car wash down on Crenshaw. He was highly connected and well-liked. Wayne showed him around, made introductions, and provided overall information about the lay of the land. He would become immensely helpful and vital to the brothers as the organization grew. However, it didn't take long for Meech to be up to his old tricks. Just as Harold complained many years before, Demetrius had a habit of not paying his debts and ruining solid business relationships.

Terry would be left to clean up his brother's mess. Whenever anyone found it difficult to collect from one, they sought out the other. In any case, it was always Terry paying a debt or smoothing over ruffled feathers. So he flew out to the West Coast and found a condo to settle into. His time was increasingly spread between California and Detroit as he fixed whatever mess his brother caused and situated himself into a better supply of product.

Harold and I slipped back into co-parenting and attempted to find an understanding of each other and a mutual way forward. Unfortunately, he would secretly grow angrier and seethe over my changed heart and the person I decided to be with. Life wasn't the same as he had left it. Marlon was now only a few months away from graduating high school, Jason was a teenager, and Corey wasn't a baby. They all had their own minds and challenged his authority and overall place in their lives as he began to push his own rules and authority upon them. I guess for him life seemed to pass him by, and he was on the verge of losing any involvement in the direction his family was headed.

"Cheapskate!" Corey yelled from the banister.

Harold undoubtedly put his foot down on some purchase; Corey, picking up my habits and repeating what he had heard from me, belched out the insult to his father as he charged to his room. It was clear my children were picking up habits I didn't want them to have and that our changing lifestyle was something Harold was unwilling to adjust to or submit to our many whims. Only God knows what went through Harold's mind as he stood there, stoic and firm in his position, before heading out the door.

* * *

*BOOM!*

The sudden impact of another vehicle colliding head-on into the driver's-side door blindsided me. My ears rang with a piercing noise as the car that was careening into mine pushed me off to the side of the road. The airbags deployed, tires skidded, and shattered glass flew everywhere as the car crashed to a halt, leaving me completely dazed and in shock. A dark figure approached and pulled at the passenger door as it screeched open. Frozen, I could just make out that my attacker was Harold. Fear ran down my spine as he balled his fist and began to strike me in the face.

The bones in my wrist cracked as I shielded myself from a devastating pummel to the face. His fist landed the occasional strike across my face. All the fear I felt rushed over me as I prayed he would stop.

Harold's face was red with fury as he took unrelenting swing after swing. It seemed unlikely he had any plans to stop—until I stopped breathing. As I tried to fight him away, I had nowhere to run. My door was blocked by his SUV, and I couldn't go anywhere or do anything except shield myself from the next strike. My children's faces flashed in my mind and what would happen to them if I didn't make it out of this alive. Screaming, I couldn't let this be the end.

Suddenly Harold stopped. His attention turned to a car slowing down and peering into my windshield to see this strike on my life. He quickly backed away and swiftly exited back out of the car and ran to his truck, before disappearing into the night. Struggling and distraught, I climbed out of my car and began to limp home, holding my numb arm and bleeding.

*"Call the police!"*

The boys screamed as I stumbled through the front door of my home and my sons looked on in horror. Corey looked through the banister as he dialed 911. I wailed in pain, unable to move, as I sank to the floor.

# SHIT HAPPENS

"Mom, what happened?" Marlon yelled.

"Harold," I gasped, hardly able to speak or string a full sentence together. I was totally out of it as Marlon stormed to the kitchen and quickly returned, brandishing a knife. "I'm gonna kill him!" exclaimed Marlon as he paced.

"My . . . my mom . . . she's been hurt." Corey trembled as he answered the questions of the dispatcher. This had to be the most horrifying scene for him to witness. His mother was badly hurt at the hands of his father—and he loved us both so much. I could only imagine the dilemma he was in as he called and reported the incident. Shortly after, the paramedics arrived and deduced that my arm was broken. I would need medical attention.

As I recovered, tears streamed from my mother's eyes as she looked on, joined by my stepfather, who both waited in my hospital room. As I lay there, I knew that had it not been for that lone stranger, I wouldn't be in a hospital bed but a body bag—and that was something to be thankful for.

"Why don't you ride to California with me?" Terry proposed.

He would suggest that a road trip and vacation would do me good during recovery. As I was on leave from work, I had more than enough time to get away from the city, plus my reluctance to be seen was another convincing reason to leave my problems behind and ride with him.

"It could do you some good to get away and clear your mind for a few days," Terry whispered soothingly in my ear as he lay with me on the night of my return home. My arm was now wrapped in a cast as it healed, and my body was still bruised. He rubbed and comforted me as I felt weak and defeated, agonizing over guilt and embarrassment at the thought of this horrific incident.

I blamed myself for Harold's rage, believing I could have done something differently or that I was somehow at fault. The feeling of guilt sat on my heart like a rock, adding pressure. I wondered, *What is it about me? What caused Harold to treat me this way? Why were my experiences with men, so far, not what I had hoped for?*

We headed south toward St. Louis, then Atlanta, where we turned west through Texas, as both Houston and Dallas would be stops along the way—a short shopping trip at the Galleria in Houston and a romantic dinner in Dallas before heading farther west. We'd stop in Vegas, where Terry would try a few hands at the blackjack table, while I would luxuriate at one of the hotel spas, then back on the road for our final destination— Los Angeles.

# Chapter 10

# Mulholland Drive

*2000 to 2003*

As Corey joined us in searching for a place to live, he began to show a keen interest in everything related to our business. I didn't give much thought about what my boys would do with their lives as much as I was concerned with them becoming well-rounded men with good values. I wanted to provide them with the best education so they wouldn't follow in my or Terry's footsteps. I wouldn't have cared if they became plumbers or car salesmen—as long as they did not sell drugs.

Nonetheless, Marlon would eventually drop out of tech school to work for Terry behind my back. His childhood friends Charles and Maurice would soon follow him into the trade. While Jason seemed to shun any commitment to the business, with little interest in academics or working for the family, he'd stick to himself mostly and developed quite a habit of smoking weed. Corey's hobby of reading young adult novels changed from Harry Potter to *Forbes, Black Enterprise,* and *Rich Dad Poor Dad* and its spin-off series. The idea of making money legitimately would take up most of his time. Even still, his affinity for making money only

79

helped to grow his own bond with Terry. They talked for hours endlessly about cars, private jets, and business subjects he read about.

"One . . . two . . . three . . ." Corey began counting faster with every crisp $100 bill that passed through his fingers. "Eight hundred, nine hundred, one thousand!" He'd take a stack of ten and cross it over another stack until it was five. Then he would shuffle them all back together, before twisting two rubber bands after another around the wads of cash, before starting the next one. That afternoon, while sitting in the CVS parking lot, we waited on Cuzzo to drop off a box of brownies—only the savory treats had been replaced with $80,000 in $100 bills. The money had been sent by Terry to cover bills, which we carefully recounted together, before heading off to handle errands.

First we stopped at a small travel agency on Ventura Boulevard. I pulled one stack away from the rest and handed it over to Corey and instructed him to go inside with my platinum American Express and inform the salesclerk he wanted to pay his credit card bill with cash. At the time, $1,000 cash was the maximum allowed without raising any red flags. Making Corey do this errand would also teach him how to pay bills on time—and that his credit was most important. Next we hit Comerica to deposit cash. I handed him a deposit slip and walked him through the steps to cover checks that would come out, including the Department of Water and Power bill, which we would do last before heading over the hill for more pressing issues.

Shopping!

During a leisurely browse through Neiman Marcus one day, I met a wealthy woman who, over her dark Chanel shades, looked me up and down, from head to toe, before remarking, "Jus' gorgeous, honey. I love the heels!"

# MULHOLLAND DRIVE

I'd repeatedly run into her in ready-to-wear at Saks; the shoe department at Barneys, where my go-to guy, Walter, would bring champagne, along with the latest stilettos by Manolo, Christian Louboutin, and Prada; then I'd head to Gucci on Rodeo, where Jason and Kelly would whisk me and Corey away to the VIP section, serving us both more champagne and Coca-Cola, respectively. Afterward, they would pull in racks of clothing and countless boxes of shoes from the new season collection. It was easy for me to drop fifty or even a hundred grand in a single shopping trip, and my spending habits brought me exclusive invitations to receive an American Express Centurion Card, also called the Black Card, and additional 20 percent discounts—not to mention being able to pull unreleased runway collections to take home and decide on before purchasing—all off the strength of my "husband" being a heavyweight himself, with links to Sean "P. Diddy" Combs.

In California, you could dream and be anybody you wanted to be. For me, that was being a stay-at-home mother and the wife of an ultra-wealthy music producer from the Midwest. Shortly after arriving, we'd gone from the suburbs of Sherman Oaks to the much tonier hillside of Bel-Air. The $3,000,000 three-story estate, just off Mulholland, would stamp out any doubt or question about the source of our wealth, let alone if it was a lie when I promptly gave my address with the zip code 90077. My neighbors included wealthy tax attorneys, NBA stars Shaquille O'Neal and Gary Payton, and revered television judge Greg Mathis. It was undeniable that I had the money, homes, and everything else that went with this charade.

Carrying over the tradition from my AAA days, an annual trip with my boys for spring break—and our first family vacation with Terry—would reflect this opulent lifestyle. Chartering a Gulfstream G500, we landed on the small island of Barbados, where a caravan of black SUVs scooped fifteen of us from the tarmac and quickly whisked us away to not any of the common all-inclusive resorts, but to one of three lavish villas, which I had booked at the behest of Terry.

"*This* is how you do a vacation. Fuck we gone stay at a hotel for and can't party and do what we want!" Terry said, bragging.

Our motorcade sped along the narrow roads overtaking the beautiful crystal blue waters, straight through a small town, where the one-and-only Popeyes stood, past the jungles into a tranquil gated neighborhood, with sprawling villas. Arriving, we pulled onto the grounds of a vanilla-white estate, with lush green gardens cooled by the shade of low-hanging branches from a stunning willow tree in the front yard.

We entered the foyer, which opened into the living area, where the doors pulled back, allowing air to flow seamlessly, while displaying a sparkling blue pool, with the ocean as a backdrop just a few yards away.

"Welcome to Barbados. I'm Akeelah," the head house manager greeted us at the entranceway, with some of the staff. They would make sure to provide us with everything we needed throughout our stay.

"Hi, I'm Toni, and this is Terry."

"May I show you both to the master bedroom?" she asked politely.

We nodded, still astonished by the place, as she led us away and up a flight of stairs. It was more breathtaking than I expected. I thought that the pictures didn't quite capture the majestic views or picturesque loft-style master bedroom, with a view overlooking the pool, and an even more mesmerizing ocean view at its elevated vantage point.

Eric and his girlfriend, Mecho, would join us at the main residence. Originally from Florida, Eric met Terry and Meech through Tara, Meech's longtime girlfriend, who was also Mecho's cousin. Eric came with the nominal amount of $50,000 cash to buy work from the brothers, which didn't impress Meech, but Terry found the money useful when he needed to shore up cash to pay creditors, much to the dismay of his brother. I had an inkling that he did it just to spite his brother, as they had a growing rivalry.

Meech disliked Eric, who was dirty and lacked teeth when we met him. He did not fit the caliber of people the brothers were normally known to associate with. For Terry, it was less a business-savvy move of recognizing a rising star, and more of a calculated one to get under his brother's skin. Nonetheless, Eric quickly climbed the ranks and became one of Terry's closest advisors.

Eric could be charming and likable, but I found him at times to be loud and obnoxious. He often caused discomfort as his influence increased over Terry's own decisions and ability to manage the ever-growing empire, which we had taken years to create and risked everything to build. Mecho, a dark chocolate–skinned girl, also from Florida, was very different. Polite and observant, she was the complete opposite of "Peaches," the girlfriend of Terry's childhood friend and second in charge, Pig.

Straight out of Atlanta, and like most women from the South, Peaches was beautiful, thick, with a heavy accent. She loved to jump around and have fun with the rest of us. Peaches also had a proclivity for other women, which would pique the interest of Erica, aka "the other Peaches."

Erica, or "Peaches," was Corey's godmother and "auntie"; she had been a younger girl from my block on Coyle Street and I took her in as a little sister when things at her own household seemed hopeless.

"Get off that porch," I'd repeatedly tell her when I would catch her outside drinking with others from the block. She would be there many times to help raise and babysit my youngest son, even till today. A closeted lesbian growing up, she now went after any female she found attractive with the same conviction as her male counterparts, which on occasion would cause tension with some of the guys. She was now an adult, and I could not tell her much, before things became heated after she made advances at Mecho, after what I like to think was a result of having too many shots of tequila.

It was because of this exchange, and some differences still unclear, that Cuzzo, enraged, stormed out to the pool deck at the other villa and tried to berate Peaches while swimming with Corey.

"What the hell you think you're doing, Peaches?"

Shocked, Peaches hesitated. "What?"

"You heard me!"

"Hey, don't talk to her like that!" Corey screamed back. Cuzzo's eyes filled with rage focused on Corey.

"Stay in a kid's place!"

Peaches grew angry that he was directing his rage at Corey. She yelled back, "Don't yell at him!"

When it got back to Terry, their argument caused a chasm of events to unfold. This turned out to be the beginning of a rift that affected our own relationship. Terry sided with Cuzzo and chided Corey, which left me slightly agitated. He was now helping to raise Corey, but even still, Peaches was a grown woman who could do what she wanted.

*Cuzzo has no authority,* I thought.

Charles, Marlon's childhood friend who had begun to work for the family, had begun harboring the same feelings and growing resentment. He would chime in one evening, "That's Tee's favorite!" Charles laughed with the group, except for Terry, or "Tee," who became visibly annoyed; then he turned and threw his own less humorous jab.

"Shut up, black-ass nigga, you a flashlight's favorite!"

Rochelle, Marlon's girlfriend from high school, cackled loudly.

"All a nigga gotta do is smile so somebody can find his black ass in the middle of nowhere," Pig added between laughing.

Charles would take the jokes about his complexion in stride, but the tensions between the pair only grew.

"Yeah, my shit sparkles like diamonds. Nigga don't even need no jewelry to pull these hoes," he concluded with his trademark bright smile.

"Black pulls them with just a smile," I interjected.

"Thanks, Auntie, you already know!" Charles chuckled.

"Me and Lil Dogg use to take all these dudes' girls. Auntie knows—"

"Yeah, all right, now," Rochelle interrupted, trying to hide her annoyance under a joking demeanor.

"Better tell them to tighten they stomach muscles!" Charles rubbed his tummy, with a huge smile that displayed his sparkling white teeth.

# Chapter 11
# Too Busy Surviving

*Corey's narration*
*2002 to 2013*

WHEN ANYONE HEARS JUST A LITTLE ABOUT MY UPBRINGING AND life, two questions always come up: What was it like? How was I able to survive?

The short answer is God, but with the utmost sincerity, I often respond by saying, "You don't know you're surviving when you are busy surviving."

Split, click . . . paste.
Play.

This was my sixteenth edit, and I would begin to feel some confidence in the sizzle reel that had become my sole responsibility to finish. My body began to feel hot as the blood in my veins pumped faster, and my head felt like a helium party balloon just before bursting, the pressure becoming heavier as the anticipation for the final cut came closer.

"Lisa B" got past my phone's Do Not Disturb setting with her repeated calls, breaking my concentration as her name appeared across the screen. It was the seventh call within the past hour, and it only made the weight of expectation greater. The sound of the buzzer grew as I tried to cut and drag the next clip into place.

Determined to get an answer, she hit redial repeatedly as her patience waned to see my final cut of the *BMF Wives* sizzle reel.

Lisa, the second lead in an ensemble cast, was a tight-lipped mix chick with attitude from Los Angeles. She had a spotted presence in my life, first appearing as my barber and shortly after came back around because of her husband, Paul Buford, who was once a member of *BMF* before disappearing again during the indictment, only to make yet another reappearance once my mother returned from federal prison. We began work to tell her story and help other at-risk women and children.

Both my mother and I have similar, comparable upbringings. I hardly knew my father growing up, for he was serving multiple sentences for drug trafficking, and I spent most of my adolescence and teenage years feeling much different than the rest of my family. My brothers have brown skin with good hair, while I am light-skinned with tight curls. My main interests centered on the *Forbes* lists, *Black Enterprise,* and tuning into CNBC faithfully, as opposed to ESPN, like my brother Marlon. Although I owned many clothes, shoes, and jewelry before I could drive, I collected model cars and bought my first vending machine. It's the furthest thing that my brothers, or any kids at my age, were interested in. Possibly because of this, I had an inkling early on that my mother and family would come to rely on me.

When we first moved to Los Angeles, I spent most of my time with my mother, so my first barber was Lisa. My mother met her at a salon in the Fairfax district, just across from the farmers' market, where she also got her hair done. Shortly thereafter, Lisa joined the hair and makeup union and transitioned into higher-paying gigs in the industry. I thought it was cool that as a teenager I had the same barber who cut my stepdad Terry's and most of the other guys' hair at home. By then, I had stopped referring to Terry as "him" and would start affectionately referring to him as "Tee" or "Pops."

At this point, Terry was the only father figure I knew, and he treated me as if I were his own son. We both loved cars, and I had an interest in the finer things in life, and we would talk endlessly about this. Unbeknownst to him, it was his actions and the things he made happen that showed and inspired me to believe anything was possible—that if I worked hard, and had enough faith, I, too, could overcome most things.

As for Lisa, she eventually reentered the picture for the second time when Terry hired her husband, Paul Buford, more commonly referred to as "PJ." Terry met PJ through Lonnie. Lonnie was a tow truck driver who came around when my mother and Tee started Oracle Motorsports, an aftermarket and auto body shop on Ventura Boulevard in Studio City, California.

I'm not sure where PJ was from exactly, but he was the typical brown-nosing thug from the inner city who began working for Tee as a "runner." This entailed fulfilling small errands, relaying messages to LA natives, hoods, gang leaders, and so forth. Most of it involved the car side of the business before evolving to include the collecting, the counting, and the dropping off of mail. "Mail" was the code word for money, or the proceeds from drug sales. PJ would transport large trash bags of money from or to one or two places—either the "Gym" or the "View," which were code names of stash houses within the county. These houses weren't your ordinary-by-day trap houses you think of; they weren't some run-down single-family flat in the ghetto. They were quite the opposite. The View was nestled in the celebrity-heavy Hollywood Hills, while the Gym was located farther down in the quiet suburb of Encino in the San Fernando Valley. Both of them were multimillion-dollar homes.

PJ was a loudmouth who talked with hubris and pretended to have a wealth of knowledge on many things. He'd only been recently released from prison. Up until then, PJ had spent most of his life in and out of jail for grand theft auto and other petty crimes. He'd never really been around anyone with access to the kinds of money he now found himself around, and he would take full advantage of this situation.

I never took a liking to PJ, even with my close relationship with Terry. Of course, I wouldn't let him know that or feel the need to tell him about PJ's need to call me "spoiled." After another relative reported his behavior to my mom, PJ would go and refer to me as a "snitch." Eventually Tee would get wind of it, just before a flight to New York, where PJ begrudgingly had taken us to the Van Nuys Airport and then disembarked to take a commercial flight, after Terry decided that he wasn't going to allow him to fly with us on our private jet.

Vacations and trips to the mall were just like everything else. I was a real-life Richie Rich. Everyone was invited along for the ride and welcome to get whatever they wanted, no questions asked. The budget was of no concern or thought. This meant not only my stepbrother, "Little Tee"; his sister, Alexis; my cousin Kevin; and, as he put it, the babysitter Bjorn—they all came along for the ride on this trip to New York.

We landed in the city with a big splash; back-to-back SUVs awaited us on the tarmac and swiftly whisked us into the city. First we stopped at the Waldorf Astoria, where my parents disembarked. Terry had already ruled that the kids would not stay here. The motorcade pulled away and dropped us off at an equally opulent hotel, at least as far as the penthouse was concerned. There we found a sundeck, with multiple floors, and 360-degree views of the city. We could see the Empire State Building looming in the distance. It was beyond what anyone could have dreamed of for a first trip to the big city, especially for me, who fantasized of one day living there, and who shared the same vision as my stepdad. I wanted to live a life just as extravagant as the one we had begun to live.

A shopping trip to Harlem for aftermarket Nikes and Air Jordans would come to a grand total of $30,000, with tourist stops at the Apollo Theater, Times Square, and front-row seats to a Knicks game. Tee would be heard on wiretaps bragging about spending between $65,000 and $85,000 for good seats, especially during the playoffs when the Lakers would win back-to-back championships. My mom and dad lived the life of the rich and famous, and we kids were treated like the offspring of some famous rapper or hip-hop star. It certainly would ring true when at the final stop we met a real hip-hop icon, "Jacob the Jeweler."

We entered the pristine white showroom where diamond rings and watches sparkled from the showcases. Just like a scene out of *Entourage,* his assistant quietly appeared from an invisible door and waved us to the back and up a flight of stairs into Jacob's personal office. Sitting behind his desk, Jacob Arabo was a tall, stern Arab man, sociable but quiet. He motioned to his assistant, who zipped out and quickly returned with a suede-covered tray filled with diamond watches and a round-cut diamond pinky ring. He put it down before us. There were Jacob watches fully flooded in diamonds, diamond and gold chains, and an Audemars Piguet watch, which Tee had dropped off on a prior trip for a repair and was now fixed.

"What y'all want?" Tee asked.

We all became giddy with excitement. I pointed at a watch like the one I already had, but instead of just having a diamond bezel, the entire casing, including the face, had been set in white diamonds. Little Tee decided on something similar, while Alexis would push her limits and choose not only a watch but a ring and tennis bracelet as well.

Alarmed, Little Tee interrupted. "You can't get all that!" he yelled at her.

"She can get what she want!" Terry overruled. "Don't worry about what she getting!"

Alexis shot a snarky glance at Little Tee, just like any other girl who'd gotten her way when Daddy said so. It wasn't just her thinking to get what she wanted, we all could. I turned in my old watch and waited for Jacob's assistant to return with the requested pieces. The jewelry, the massive amounts of money spent on clothes and homes, would embroil my mother, along with Jacob, as co-conspirators in a money-laundering case involving the undocumented expenditures on this very trip and much more spent, including the lingering debts, of which Tee and Eric stayed behind to work out the details.

From there, the rest of the kids decided we should hit Junior's, a restaurant in Brooklyn known for its cheesecake. It became a staple after being featured on MTV'S *Making the Band,* featuring P. Diddy. Similar to what happened on the show, the driver Tee had arranged to chauffeur us around would leave us stranded with thousands of dollars' worth of jewelry. So there we were trying our best to hail a cab in the undesirable part of town.

This happily-ever-after life in California wouldn't last forever and it would come crumbling down around us a few years later. Persuaded by seeing my mom go against her better judgment, and quickly regret the act of putting the White House compound deed into her name, this real estate decision would lead to her eventual indictment, along with seventeen other members who have become known as the Black Mafia Family, or just BMF. While leaving me in the dark, my mom would be sentenced to fifty-seven months in a federal prison, and she'd leave me and my older brother Jason practically to our own devices. We were forced to grow up and learn to survive on our own. This life would be in stark contrast to the once-posh lifestyle we had grown accustomed to and damn near reliant on.

# BLACK MAFIA QUEEN

At the age of eighteen, I discovered it wasn't always easy surviving and juggling work and school. In the mornings, I attended California State University, Northridge, or CSUN; then in the afternoon, I commuted to the Universal Music Group offices in Santa Monica for my second internship in the music industry. In the evenings, I wrapped, packed, and shipped marijuana with my best friend, Langston. On the weekends, I'd party and leave my hungover friends at my apartment while I took an hour-long drive up to Victorville to visit my mom. That was usually on Saturdays and an occasional Sunday as well.

I spent my days doing turnaround trips to Michigan to pick up cash I made from the week before, only to repeat the cycle every week. Burning the candle on both ends would seem exasperating in hindsight, but I was truly high off the adrenaline—or at least driven by the youth and excitement from coming of age in my own right. My oldest brother, Marlon, was also sentenced to eleven years in a federal prison, which left me wanting to step in as a dad to my first niece, Malana, often taking her to do the extracurricular activities that I enjoyed as a child. We would visit the Getty Museum or go see the circus when I could, and her mom would allow it. I also put into practice the tools I had learned about being responsible from the lessons my mom had taught me. Paying my bills, credit cards, car expenses, and my brothers on time left little room for error or the allowance to make mistakes that most teens and young adults can make early on.

As for my brother Jason, he and I were polar opposites, like night and day. He started smoking and drinking in his early teens and preferred hood bars and block parties frequently seen between Crenshaw Boulevard and Inglewood, while I tended to hang with my friends who went to USC and UCLA. I hung out with frat boys, collegiate athletes, and attended parties in the Hills and went to exclusive invitation-only clubs with Saudis. These are the places I preferred because it was a way of staying connected to the best parts of our past life, only realizing later the change affected Jason much harder than any of us realized, leading him to spiral out of control years later.

Serious doubts over my chosen major and career path began to creep in from the strain of working and balancing home life, which would eventually lead to my suspension after failing economics twice. I was required to attend a junior college to pick up my grade, but subsequently would be suspended because of a petty dispute over a parking spot, which resulted in me having a scuffle with another student. Not only did we have a class together, he and I had been paired into groups after not being able to convince our professor that we should be kept apart.

I was forced to pull out of the class and therefore became disenchanted with the idea of graduating; instead, I focused on finding a new path, while drifting more into selling weed with Langston. However, this, too, would be curtailed when Jason moved in with me and left Langston in a bind. Unaware that Jason was spending money recklessly and not paying his rent finally caught up with him, family responsibilities would fall once again on me out of obligation. I had to allow him and his girlfriend to live with me, which blindsided Langston. This news undoubtedly fractured our friendship and fledging partnership.

Langston was my first faithful friend outside the family, and I would clamp on to him for familiarity. In many ways, I was both inspired by and learned a lot from him. It was his influence that pushed and ignited a fire in me to make things happen and to keep a hustle going, which would be the influence I needed to keep my apartment when things began to change financially for us. Now, fully supporting my brother as well meant a strain on the funds I made; and now being a college dropout meant no financial aid or any other supplemental support to count on. From this point on, things became hard, but it was the ingenuity of my friend that helped me have the drive to keep a roof over my head so that my mother could be released into my custody.

# BLACK MAFIA QUEEN

*   *   *

Life had drastically changed with the absence of my mom, and with the majority of the family either in prison as well, or thousands of miles away back in Detroit. The moment she was released, it became apparent that life had changed. The many friends we had before had deserted us.

We went from having multiple cars at our disposal to just one car; and with the loss of another million-dollar townhome, we had no choice but to share my two-bedroom college apartment. It took a tremendous effort to adjust and reacquaint ourselves with the woman we thought we knew. And now my mother would have to accept the fact that her sons were both adults. We no longer frequented fancy restaurants or spent exorbitant amounts of money on clothes. Instead, we applied for food stamps and did the surveys on the back of our Popeyes receipts to receive the free chicken when money was short, or we wanted to eat out.

We sold many of the clothes, jewelry, and other objects left in storage to make ends meet and survive before my mom would urge me to go back to school and do something with my life. Determined not to make the same mistakes as my eldest brother had made, I acknowledged the love of film I had and tapped into my dream of wanting to become a writer. I enrolled in the Los Angeles Film School, or LAFS.

It was through film school endeavors, and navigating my own struggles to pursue my dreams, that my mother and I became inspired to co-found Sylent Heart, a foundation to help children with incarcerated parents. Using this vehicle, my mom shared her plight as a woman in order to deter young at-risk girls from following the same path she had, and to find their own voices, instead. It was the beginning of the perfect combination to begin our journey in telling her story for the purpose of helping others, while giving us both a platform: me to write, and her to work with others inside and outside the prison system.

# Chapter 12

# Divided We Fall

*2003*

Cracks began to show in Terry and Meech's relationship by the start of 2003. Slowly, dissension would make its way through the ranks and affect the overall operation of the business. Those who stood to gain from a separation promoted a growing animosity and hastened the breaking up of the operation into factions in order to increase their own pockets and material wealth. I could see early on that this would become a cause for disaster and would wreak more havoc as the brothers became more of a check and balance for each other. One without the other left them both open to making careless mistakes and other reckless behavior, which could get us all sent to prison—or so I believed.

Early on, I went to Tara and asked for her help in getting the brothers to speak, but it fell on deaf ears. "Girl, Meech done bought and did more for me than he ever has," she responded calmly after a phone call in which I pleaded with her to see things my way. It was for nothing, because Tara wanted the same useless shit I had, or so I thought. Shoes, bags, and jewelry—none of this would mean anything if the Feds hauled us all to jail. I couldn't make her see that.

Tara, a pretty brown-skinned girl from Florida, was Meech's longtime girlfriend. When it came to family events, the holidays, and vacations, most of the guys preferred to bring the most important woman in their lives around, leaving the side chicks for other times. Meech was no different, and since Tara was the main woman in his life, and the soon-to-be mother of his child, she could hold the most sway when it came to his decisions. However, it also only seemed to help make him vie to have more control, instead of Terry. Making sly remarks about his weight and other comments I mostly ignored, it became abundantly clear, especially after a summer trip across the ocean, that she didn't like her beau's brother and had no qualms about it.

"Aye, babe," Terry called after me as I lay across my sofa in my walk-in closet, packing for another trip to New York.

"Puff just called," he continued. "He said how much fun it was last summer meeting Corey and your mom, and we should come back this year."

During the past summer, Corey, my mother, and I, all sharing an interest in traveling, took a European tour across Italy and France to celebrate our birthdays. We ended up ditching the tour, once we got to Nice, France, and disembarked in a taxi to Saint-Tropez to meet up with hip-hop heavyweight Sean Combs—Terry still called him "Puff."

Upon returning to the States, I raved about it to Terry nonstop, and was quite sure he had a fear of missing out again. This invitation from Puff made him pull out all the stops to make sure this trip was even more grand and unforgettable: shelling out $500,000 for private chartered jets, both Meech's and our room on board the megayacht we would sail the Mediterranean on, and whatever else Puff sent the bill for. It's unclear if anyone else put in a dime including Mr. Combs himself.

Puff, Terry, and Meech were close. Terry talked on the phone almost daily with the now-embattled hip-hop icon. Terry would become a confidant to Puff during and after the shooting at a nightclub that led subsequently to a criminal trial, which also involved the artist Shyne. It affected Puff both professionally and personally. We all stood in his corner until, in a twist of fate, he was acquitted of all the charges; if he had been found guilty, it would have been Puff's downfall. Through the ups and downs, remaining steadfast in his corner, Terry and Meech came close to being the financial backers of the clothing line Sean John before Ron Burkle and a bevy of other legitimate businessmen stepped in and took the risk when Puff himself wasn't so confident about his name carrying a full-on streetwear brand.

Leaving Corey behind, and joining Meech and Tara in New York, my cousin Cato and one of Terry's friends named Mike, from back home, would meet us at a party Puff was throwing before we were set to leave the next day. While exiting the club, we would catch wind that the "hip-hop police" had been at the party and were going to tail us back to our hotel. Mike fucked with them, driving in circles and running several red lights, before we finally made it to our room. I wondered if it was the hip-hop police still having a bone to pick for having lost the case against Puff or if the DEA was really behind it. I'd quickly shove the idea deep down in my thoughts.

The next day, we, along with fifty other close friends and associates of Sean's, boarded a Boeing business jet to Marrakesh. Tommy Lee, Naomi Campbell, Carl Thomas, along with a host of other A-list actors, musicians, and business leaders, joined us on this nonstop flight of partying from takeoff to landing in the North African country of Morocco. Even his music videos, which displayed all his wealth, could not compare to the extravagance we experienced once we were on the ground in Morocco.

Fitting right into our made-up Hollywood fairy tale, Terry and I high-sided with the A-list celebrities and rubbed shoulders with billionaires and world leaders; we drank copious amounts of champagne and tequila, smoked weed, popped other illicit drugs, and partied throughout the night.

I was also reminded to feel gratitude for the life we lived—and for being an American, unlike the less fortunate in these undeveloped countries who had to deal with extreme poverty and starvation. As we departed into the towns in large caravans, tour guides would warn us not to give the beggars any money. Even still, the pain in many of their eyes would be unbearable to witness, so someone would break from this warning and hand over a few dollars. Some of the beggars did come close to toppling over one of the vans as we passed through their little village after shopping. The locals started pressing the sides of our vehicles, almost scaring me into praying for safety, unsure what would happen if we crashed and they bombarded us. Eventually we arrived at a stunning castle, where we all stayed, including Puff and Kim Porter, his longtime girlfriend.

There I would get acquainted with Sheikh Saad, who was impressed with our demeanor and wanted to get to know us better.

"Come have dinner at my home this evening," he said enchantingly.

This invite did not include Puff, or any of the other celebrities that the sheikh already knew, or he could have extended his grace to; instead, it was just given to Terry and myself. I excitedly went to inform Tee about it while he was resting in our guest room.

"Let's just go, me and you!" I tried to persuade him.

Although I was thinking in our best interest, it became clear that he didn't see it that way, nor did he think as highly of us as a couple. Instead, Terry became enraged.

"Sack chaser!" he yelled.

Alarmed, I froze as he jumped into a tirade. "You're a fuckin' gold digger, stupid bitch!" he continued.

We argued until it was time to head to the dinner, and Puff surely joined us and stole the show. Terry shrunk under his bombastic showmanship; and to this day, I ponder if I should have kept it to myself and gone alone. It could've just been fatigue from all the travel, as every couple on the trip at some point wound up getting into a shouting match or, worse, a full-on brawl, including Puff and Kim.

After departing Morocco, we set sail on the Mediterranean on a megayacht that was bigger than most party boats, where a fight between the star couple would end in blows. Kim would end up with a broken nose, which tabloids covered as a fall while on the boat deck. This combative atmosphere would linger over to Tara and Meech, who decided to end the trip early so he could rush back to Atlanta to sneak around with a girl named Sugar. Meanwhile, we stayed to continue the vacation.

Helicopters swooped us up from the yacht and transported us over to Ibiza, the small Spanish island known for its intense parties and raves. The partying only intensified once we converged on a sprawling estate on its own secluded island. There was no way in or out, other than by boat or helicopter. Ibiza was perfectly tucked away from prying eyes and the paparazzi lenses that swarmed us. I knew Puff was addicted to drugs after he'd pestered Terry about not having any ecstasy while in Miami. My cousin Cato had to find him some, under any circumstance, back then; but here, hidden away from gossipmongers, it would hit extreme levels of no breaks, in between three days of no sleep. Many, including Puff, would fully undress and run off into a cave where the DJ played music, without abandon; and my head began to spin in pain, hardly able to keep my eyes open. I couldn't take another moment. I thought I could hang with the best of them, but I came to realize I was wrong.

Packing my things up, I told Tee it was now our turn to leave, but that was damn near impossible on this tiny island. With the party host incoherent and preoccupied, matters were made even worse with the huge language barrier that caused the task to be nearly impossible. We were finally able to charter a helicopter back to the Spanish coast and caught a jet to London.

Finally, away from the private chefs and catering services serving the traditional foods of whatever country we were in—and dying for some familiarity—we hopped in a cab and, through a complicated hand signal and broken English translation, conferred with the driver to take us to the closest KFC, which was actually nowhere close. We had to go to a rough part of town for some good ole fried chicken.

"Don't you want to put that up and put on shoes?" I asked Terry.

Frowning, Tee responded, "Shit, real recognize real." Against my advice, he kept on his Gucci slides, along with his diamond encrusted Audemars Piguet watch, pinky ring, and diamond chain, implying that regardless of where we were, even the most hood gangsters could recognize another one of their own and he was safe to do as he pleased. Still hesitant, I put my jewelry away and we entered and ordered, without incident, a pair of two-piece meals.

"Let's go shopping," Tee said abruptly as we got back in the cab before telling the driver where to go. I figured it was his attempt to make up for the way he acted while in Morocco and I'd accept it, knowing he always made up for his behavior and cheating by buying me lavish gifts.

Without hesitation, I turned to the driver and said, "Hermès store!"

The Birkin bags were highly sought-out purses by the rich and famous, but were hard to obtain back in the States. After seeking one out from West Coast to East Coast, I had waited for this overseas trip to finally get one. I knew the flagship store would have a variety of options to choose from. This would be my moment— like straight out of *Pretty Woman*—knowing he would spend whatever amount of money for me to ignore his words and even more severe actions. When it came to asking forgiveness, it wasn't so much a verbal apology, but rather the amount spent—and Terry was prepared to go the extra mile.

The store was warm and inviting, with beautiful displays of their trademark scarves and throw blankets, but the staff exhibited a much colder energy when this little Black girl first entered. They stared with little emotion, wondering if perhaps I had walked into the wrong boutique or wasn't in the right neighborhood. I was made to feel as though I was someone's nanny who had come in to remind the missus that it was time to fetch their children from school.

"Hello, is there something I can help you with?" the plumpish gray-haired sales associate asked in her heavy Cockney accent.

"Yes, I'm looking for your Birkins?"

Without so much as giving it a second to think, she responded, "We've got none." The sales associate spoke with little interest, not even bothering to offer to show me anything else in the store. Even though I was dressed in designer clothing, but without a drop of jewelry except for diamond stud earrings, she had already assessed that either I couldn't afford it or was not the type of clientele Hermès wished to have near their other goods. I refused to let her decide and so I politely responded, "Thank you." I gazed around the showroom once more before disappearing back out onto the street to find Terry waiting.

He chuckled as I recounted the treatment that I had just received moments before.

"Yeah, you a nigga!" he quipped.

"*What?*" Astounded by his brutal honesty, I felt a bit of rage inside at his calm demeanor, because down deep inside, I knew he was right.

"How many Black women come into their store to buy a twenty-five-thousand-dollar handbag? Even if you got money, you still a nigga, bey. Come on!" Terry called back to me as he marched toward the store. Flinging the heavy brass entrance doors open, he began to rummage through his messenger bag before pulling out two wads of cash.

"Hello, monsieur, looking for anything in particular?" It was the same rosy-cheeked woman whose snobbish demeanor had suddenly vanished into a pleasant smile.

"Yeah, my wife wants one of your Birkin bags."

"Of course." She scurried away quickly, while signaling another young girl for aid. After a brief absence, they returned with an assortment of choices, in color and size, shooting glances of disregard toward me and the encounter that had just taken place beforehand with us. They didn't give a shit about how I felt, but they waited on him, hand and foot.

Either way, I had the last laugh, with a smile on my face, as they handed me two beautifully wrapped Birkin bags. One was an oversized camel color, and the other was black; both were boxed in the trademark Hermès orange boxes and carefully placed in the same hue shopping bag. I suddenly knew exactly how Julia Roberts's character Vivian Ward must have felt as the saleswomen begrudgingly watched me strut out with merchandise worth $50,000.

By now, Terry and Meech controlled a network of more than eleven states, from New York, Georgia, Texas, California, and Missouri, which included access to multimillion-dollar mansions in each state, more than five hundred foot soldiers, and over two thousand kilos per month of 90 percent pure cocaine, supplied by two rival Mexican cartels. These drug enemies would partner up just to fulfill the brothers' demand at a drastically low price of $9,000 per kilo, where it would be sold to street dealers at $17,000 per kilo.

Yet, reaching the pinnacle of success in the streets wouldn't be enough. Enthralled in this hip-hop lifestyle, and surrounded by our celebrity friends, the lust for more grew and they became

dead set on taking the music business by storm. Demetrius especially aspired to be in the spotlight, and by most accounts wanted
to go out with a bang. He became infatuated with stardom, and
his antics began to unnerve Terry and others within the family.

Initially there would be Stomping Ground Ubiquitous. At first,
it seemed a legitimate label, with a roster of burgeoning rappers
who went by the stage name Dutch and a rising actor named Bleu
Davinci, who possessed the lesser skill set at writing, but had just
as much showmanship as Demetrius himself. Grammy Award–
winning Poo Bear and Jagged Edge, at the tail end of their record
deals, were also interested in signing on the roster; but with little
knowledge of the business, and still unsure of the name, Meech's
enterprise would lead nowhere.

It wouldn't be until a short time later, while out in Houston,
when we all returned from a trip to Cancun that the name "Black
Mafia Family" was birthed. It sprouted from a fateful newspaper
clip out of Miami that would give rise to a shadowy movement at
the time, and the beginning of both the end of a movement and
a legacy.

"Yo, we in the news!" "Big Way," another one of Terry's associates from back home, would burst into the kitchen of our Houston town house that evening. I labored over a hot skillet of turkey
chops, which were frying in cooking grease, while Terry sat at the
dining table, joined by Marlon, Pig, Meech, and Cuzzo, reading
from a message on his phone:

**Following the event P. Diddy hosted, yet another star-studded
bash he arrived with an entourage that included a large mob of men
all dressed in black many of them decked in diamond studded chains
and watches and arriving in a motorcade of exotic cars and trucks
left bystanders wondering who the mysterious group was.**

"Ha! That's right, nigga! The mob!" Pig shouted in response as
he chuckled.

"The black mafia!" said Meech, with a mischievous smirk on
his face.

"That's it!" Marlon interjected.

Terry's eyes centered on Marlon and his reaction was one of bewilderment.

*"What?"* Marlon cocked his head to the side, while turning his lip up, and then mustered out his best Godfather impression, uttering, "The Black Mafia Family!"

Meech's smirk turned into a full grin before finishing, "Entertainment."

I attended Burns Elementary School
and am six years old in this picture.
*Photo Credit: Family photo.*

Vhen I was seven years old,
lived on Coyle Street in Detroit,
Michigan, with my parents
d brothers.
*hoto Credit: Carol Thomas.*

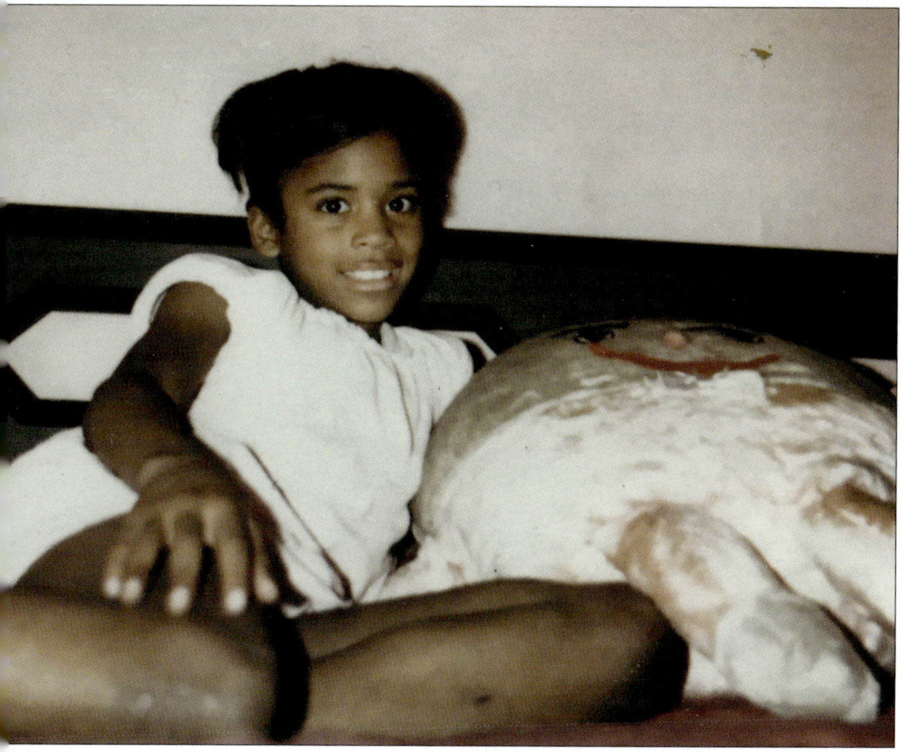

I graduated from Cooly High School at the age of seventeen. My mother Carol is on the left and my auntie Bernadette on the right. They both attended my graduation.
*Photo Credit: Family photo.*

Having a great time at a nightclub in Detroit, Michigan, during my early twenties with my best friend, Carol Turner.
*Photo Credit: Darry Welch.*

After having attended a downtown campaign event for former Mayor Eric Garcetti in downtown Los Angeles, I stopped for a photo op in front of City Hall.
*Photo Credit: H. Corey Mills.*

This photo of me at the age of nineteen was taken for a Jet magazine contest.
*Photo Credit: Carol Thomas.*

On October 25, 1992,
I married Harold Mills.
*Photo Credit: Carol Thomas.*

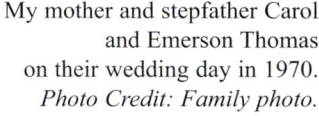

My mother and stepfather Carol
and Emerson Thomas
on their wedding day in 1970.
*Photo Credit: Family photo.*

Me and my oldest son Marlon Welch
when he was six months old.
*Photo Credit: Family photo.*

My son Marlon Welch,
on his way to his first concert
at the age of five.
*Photo Credit: Tonesa Welch.*

My youngest son, Harold Corey Mills.
*Photo Credit: Family photo.*

Here I am spending quality time
with my son Jason, who was
six years old at the time.
*Photo Credit: Family photo*

Me and my sons, Marlon Welch (12), Jason Welch (8), and Harold Corey Mills (4) while we were on a Carnival Cruise.
*Photo Credit: Carnival Cruise ship photo.*

My ex-husband Harold Mills and me at my mother's house on Coyle Street in Detroit, Michigan, with our sons, Marlon, Jason, and Corey.
*Photo Credit: Carol Thomas.*

This photo was taken circa 2000 at a hotel in New York.
From left to right: Magic (deceased), me, my youngest son Harold Corey Mills, and P. Diddy.
*Photo Credit: Christopher Triplett.*

Me with my younger son, Harold Corey Mills (left), and nephew, Darry (Shag) Price Welch (right) in 201.
*Photo Credit: Photographer Unknown, random person off the streets.*

These are the living and dining room areas of my home on Mulholland Drive.
*Photo Credit: Tonesa Welch.*

My home in Studio City, California.
*Photo Credit: Tonesa Welch.*

This is the Aston Martin car that Terry bought me for my birthday.
We saw it in a movie starring Halle Berry, and Terry wanted me to have it.
*Photo Credit: H. Corey Mills.*

Corey and I are about to board a private plane at the Van Nuys, California airport.
*Photo Credit: Tonesa Welch.*

This is me at my going away party held the night before I headed off to prison the next morning, November 7, 2008.
*Photo Credit: Jason Welch.*

This is me jumping into my friend's Rolls Royce on Ventura Blvd., while enjoying a night out on the town after coming home from prison in 2012.
*Photo Credit: H. Corey Mills.*

Me, Kim Porter, and Latarra Eutsey
during a trip to Mexico in 2003.
*Photo Credit: Phil Robinson.*

Me and my mother, Carol Thomas,
at the Fox Theater where we attended
a concert in 1992.
*Photo Credit: Fox Theater
Photographer.*

My mother Carol Thomas
and me at a family function.
I was twenty-one years old
at the time.
*Photo Credit: Emerson Thomas.*

Me and my best friend,
Carol Turner, having a great
time at a nightclub in 1991.
*Photo Credit: Photographer
unknown.*

Me with actress Lela Rochon at Sinbad's Music Soul Festival held in Aruba in 1995.
*Photo Credit: Carol Turner.*

I threw Terry Flenory a birthday party in Las Vegas at the Hard Rock Hotel in 2004.
*Photo Credit: H. Corey Mills.*

Me, Erica Johnson, and a friend in a private jet heading to New York in 2003.
*Photo Credit: H. Corey Mills.*

Terry Flenory (Southwest T) and P. Diddy hanging out in Morocco, North Africa in 2003.
*Photo Credit: Tonesa Welch.*

# Chapter 13
# Three Letters

*2003*

"**S**TAY UNDER THE RADAR," TEE WOULD URGE MEECH CONstantly.

Despite repeated warnings spurred on by my own experiences to convince him the importance of staying low-key, Terry's insistence fell on deaf ears. Demetrius grew more defiant and less inclined to listen to advice, and his own brother's opinion, as time went by. Their once-close brotherly relationship began to fall apart as Meech became more and more distant; animosity grew with every move he made. Terry's unease would be on full display to other members—and when Meech caught wind of this, it only made matters worse.

Demetrius was increasingly being referred to as "Big Meech" and gaining a reputation for spending hundreds of thousands of dollars in a single night at Atlanta strip clubs, such as Magic City and Onyx. This would be coined later on as "making it rain" by the media and rap artists alike. He also filmed and distributed the *Smack* DVD, which would go on to create a cultlike following; it featured his lone solo artist, Bleu Davinci. Bleu, a second-rate rapper, grew increasingly more involved in the street business rather than focusing on the music. He brandished guns, showed large sums of money on camera, and boasted about the illicit gains from drugs, before cutting to Meech, who stood outside his mansion with a lineup of foreign cars, invoking others to join the family in promoting and selling drugs to anyone who was able to obtain the video. It felt like a complete disaster.

*What was either one of them thinking when they made it?* I thought.

BMF was not only an acronym for "Black Mafia Family," but also for "Big Meech Flenory," and rightfully so. The attention would fall less on it being a label, but more so on the dealings and lifestyle of its CEO. The music became buried underneath the rhetoric as magazine articles featured Meech, who further implicated himself, and everyone else he was involved with, in the drug trade.

Meech incorporated BMF Entertainment and co-founded *The Juice* magazine and plastered billboards proclaiming the world was BMF's across the Atlanta skyline. It was an audacious plan to promote and push the legitimacy of the family businesses, but it would elicit more trouble; and things would take a drastic turn when a simple miscommunication outside the nightclub Club Chaos would turn violent.

Dozens of gunshots rang out on the early morning of November 13, 2003, leaving two men dead, one of which was Puff's longtime friend and head of security, Anthony "Wolf" Jones, and his associate. Meech would be injured as well, with a gunshot wound to his buttocks, and subsequently was hit with two counts of murder. He was released under police supervision pending the investigation.

Despite previously partying together in Morocco, Wolf seemingly became enraged that a woman he knew had dealings with Meech; he approached Meech, out of what appeared to be jealousy. This act swiftly turned into an altercation and, unfortunately, guns were pulled out. To this day, it's still unclear who actually took the shot during the melee, but Wolf was pronounced dead at the scene. Although the charges were eventually dropped, the high-profile case caused undue attention and the rift between the brothers widened, while causing some of our friends and associates in the industry, including Sean Combs, to draw some distance.

In Los Angeles, Terry would make inroads on his own ideas and plans to get a label off the ground and further push for legitimacy. Due to all the heat and the arrests of family and associates, he would go further to prepare for the inevitable. Inclined to launder more funds and produce legitimate income, he would be inspired by Marc Laidler, a business associate from Los Angeles, who is co-founder of the once synonymous with rims and celebrity-heavy clientele, 310 Motoring. Already having experience with my own VIP concierge and transportation service in Detroit, Terry would enlist me to help establish Oracle Motorsports, a full auto body and aftermarket automotive shop in Studio City, California. It was located just minutes from Hollywood and from the backlots of major studios, such as Universal and Warner Brothers.

We considered it a good investment for not only the cash-heavy aspect of the business, but being able to utilize the resources in-house to build stash spots in the automobiles used to transport cash and drugs. This made it easier to watch those outside the family who held the knowledge that they even existed. It also provided a vital pipeline of high-end clientele, made up of sports stars and entertainers, coming through the door.

The bevy of new connections would draw ties with the production of *CSI* to MTV's *Punk'd* and bolster Terry's intentions to appear as a legitimate businessman and create an avenue to pursue his musical pursuits. Music producers and executives would begin to clamor for a myriad of favors and financial assistance, outside of the day-to-day services of Oracle, including Kim Kardashian's first husband, multiplatinum, award-winning impresario, Damon Thomas.

One evening just before closing, Lonnie stopped in the showroom with an excited look on his face. Lonnie was an associate who quickly became a friend after providing services as a tow truck driver for not only our bevy of cars, but for the customers we provided services to as well. Our relationship became further involved as he steadily brought introductions to other high-profile clients. Corey hardly noticed him as he steadily loaded soda and Gatorade into his new vending machine, which Terry bought for him after being motivated to start his own business after having read and taken to heart the book *Rich Dad Poor Dad.* Terry reclined in a desk chair, chatting loudly with an associate over the phone, while I peered out the window to see Lonnie heading straight to our office.

"I got this dude Damon on his way. Cool cat, he's a producer," Lonnie said in a persuasively laidback tone.

Terry nodded before quizzically responding, "Okay, what's up with 'em?"

Lonnie swayed back and forth as if looking for the right words, careful not to reveal too much or say the wrong thing. "I think he can help with the music shit and point you in the right direction." Careful not to oversell or put too much hope in the meeting, he was obviously mindful of the fact that it either wouldn't come cheap or Damon had his own motives for wanting to meet as well.

Suddenly we heard the load engine hum of Damon's cherry-red 360 Spider Ferrari as he pulled directly in front of the entrance doors.

"Whoa!" Corey exclaimed in the lobby as he hopped from behind the open vending machine and headed outside to get a better look.

# THREE LETTERS

Damon, a dark-skinned, bald-headed charismatic guy from Missouri, climbed out from the driver's seat. Decked in Chrome Hearts jewelry, a leather vest, and Ed Hardy hat and shirt, he grinned as we came to greet him.

"Hello, how y'all doing?"

"Good, good!" Terry responded, in between his trademark chuckle. Lonnie turned back to look at me as I approached.

"Damon, this my people, Terry and his wife, Toni," Lonnie announced.

Corey, refusing to be left out, chimed in, "And Corey!"

"What's up, big man?" Damon replied as he gave Corey a dap on the knuckles.

"Nice ride!"

"Thanks, you like it?"

Corey nodded yes in response as he gawked at the drop-top roadster, as if he had never seen one before. He was sold. Corey immediately took a liking to Damon, and both Terry and I did as well.

Just as Terry had motives beyond music, Damon didn't come to talk cars. Despite being an extremely successful producer who raked in millions, due to his own irresponsible financial habits from living a lavish lifestyle and a looming divorce, he had fallen into debt. Contrary to the streets, many musicians, actors, and so on must live with a financial cycle. Work gets done, check gets cut, and then there's a waiting period before the next payday. It becomes vital to manage and budget until the next royalty payment, or else it spells disaster. Not nearly broke, but cash strapped, similar to Michael Jackson or Mike Tyson at one point, many talented artists scramble to shore up cash. Damon, just the same way, found himself scrambling and became vulnerable to Terry, who, in turn, took full advantage of his predicament.

On the other hand, Damon was having differences at home with his young wife, Kim. Kim was having a soon-to-be-scandalous affair with R&B crooner Ray J, the little brother of singer Brandy,

**109**

and Damon wanted the fling to end. He would come to enlist Terry's aid in discouraging Ray J in seeing Kim anymore, but Terry later turned it into another opportunity to befriend the bad-boy singer, even going as far as to let him drive his brand-new Bentley Flying Spur. In the same instance, he loaned Damon nearly $1,000,000 and reassured him not to worry about repayment in cash, provided he consult on a new label Terry was eager to start, with the addition of allowing Corey to shadow and learn the business. Tee wanted to foster my youngest son's ambitions to become a producer.

Damon happily obliged, stating excitedly, "That boy gone be rich, he something!" Damon saw potential in Corey early on, which helped my son see firsthand that his dreams of making a living legitimately were attainable.

Terry would further entrap Damon in our world when he instructed him to claim over two million dollars' worth of jewelry. After a routine stop, which resulted in Terry being arrested, the police confiscated the jewelry he was traveling with. He made a call to Damon, where through wiretap Tee could be overheard advising him to take ownership of the pieces, under the guise they were borrowed for a music video shoot, which would cause the music producer to be further implicated in a conspiracy to money launder for the family. Hesitant, Damon still went and filed a claim that he purchased the pieces from Jacob Arabo and was entitled to having them returned.

# Chapter 14

# Secret Lover

*2003 to 2005*

T ERRY'S MANIPULATION BEGAN TO SHOW NO BOUNDS. "YOU CAN'T get in trouble for spending some of my money," he said convincingly.

Even though I wasn't directly involved in the drug deals, I was unaware that I could still be prosecuted for money laundering for just spending the proceeds. In time, I would grow wearier when pressured into signing yet another million-dollar home in my name. It would be my naivete that tricked me into believing him; after all, Terry was my friend and protector—at least, that is what I told myself.

"If anything happens, I'll take the rap," he said softly before caressing my back and giving me a kiss, lowering my defenses. Even though I allowed him to sway my paranoia away, we hadn't been seeing eye to eye on most things.

Still, I knew even with my high credit score, my income couldn't justify the purchase of this extravagant house. Once again, I flew to Georgia and processed a quick deed of the compound that came to be known as the White House into my name. Nestled away in an Atlanta suburb, the estate was falling into disrepair after Meech abandoned it when a few shoddy renovations were left unfinished by unreliable contractors, who collected their payments before completing the job.

The double life, his cheating—Tee kept me on board with gifts, but not with the love I needed. Although my greed and feeling of invincibility went hand in hand, in the back of my mind, I also knew it was only a matter of time before the Feds would be on my ass again over how I was living. Forget the extravagant parties, invites to fashion shows, hanging out with celebs, renting yachts, and flying in private jets all over the world. Mind damaged, soul empty, I was drifting from day to day—and angry at my therapist for making me madder about my childhood. What about the present? Shit on top of shit, it just kept piling up. When my mom got really ill, and I had to tell her my brother had been stabbed to death in a fight with his new wife, I felt my whole life spiraling out of control.

On the chilly morning of October 31, 2003, my brother Darry, a recovering addict who had just returned home to his new wife, who was also still suffering from addiction, would get into a shouting match. The arguing turned physical over her rampant drug use. She took a kitchen knife and stabbed him directly in the heart. He stumbled from his apartment, down the stairs, before tumbling to the ground on the frigid cement and succumbing to his wounds. My nephew Darry called and woke me up to break the news. I was then forced to call my mother and inform her. She shouted in agony that her son was gone, and I screamed in pain that my best friend, the man who taught me how to ride bikes and hop fences, was gone.

"Corey, Jason, wake up. Your uncle died," Terry would call to my sons from the long hallway.

Even with him being there, Terry didn't comfort me the way I expected. Actually, it was quite the opposite. He acted cold and aloof. I reasoned that it was because during my brother's addiction, Terry's gold presidential Rolex came up missing and all reasoning pointed to him. Regardless, I experienced immense pain and anguish. I had fully expected the man I chose to be with, and the reason I put my life and freedom on the line, to have shown more compassion, but I turned a blind eye. He was absent during the arrangements of the funeral, picked meaningless fights with me, and left the repast early, with justifications that business called. According to him, he wanted to make sure we were comfortable, but it wouldn't be business that was stealing away his attention.

I had my ideas about his philandering ways, but I wasn't sure just how low he would go until things became heated down in Dallas. Marlon came charging into our home with a loaded pistol, fuming and shouting at Terry.

"I'm gone kill you!" Tears streamed from his eyes, and he trembled as he held the gun up, pointing at Terry. Terry's once-chipper mood quickly evaporated as Pig, Big Way, and I looked on, stunned.

My mind raced at the thought of Marlon pulling the trigger and my firstborn spending the rest of his life in prison, before ever grasping the idea that in an instant the man I loved would also wind up dead. I didn't try to find the reason for this seemingly out-of-nowhere rage; instead, I jumped in between them and attempted to reach for the gun.

"What's wrong, Marlon? What's going on?" I asked.

"He knows what he's doin'!" Marlon responded as he tried to nudge me away.

"Come on, let's just talk this out."

"Just calm down, son," Tee said calmly. His demeanor was relaxed, but alert.

"I'm *not* your son!" Marlon screamed back. "He thinks he can run behind my back, and I won't find out!" Marlon's eyes were bloodshot from being so irate, but slowly he began to lower the weapon.

Terry kept quiet, not saying much. I'm sure he was aware of what Marlon was referring to, but it would take time before I'd come to know the truth.

"You don't want to do this, li'l bro, just chill!" Pig chimed in as he grabbed Marlon reassuringly by the shoulder and reached for the gun.

Marlon handed the gun over and rushed back out the door, without saying a word, leaving Dallas and traveling straight back to Los Angeles that night. He didn't share with me the reason for his outburst. In retrospect, I was too afraid to ask, or deep down I already knew that Terry was communicating with Rochelle, my son's then-girlfriend and mother of his child.

Rochelle was quite literally a little girl when I first met her. Raised by her adoptive grandmother on the West Side of Detroit off Joy Road, she became like a daughter to me. She'd mimic my style, and I would take her to get her nails done and teach her how to dress. I bought Rochelle her first pair of Gucci heels, and she practically moved into my Southfield home before we ultimately moved to Los Angeles.

This was before she and Marlon got their first apartment together. She was, and would forever be, family when we got the breaking news she was pregnant with my first grandchild, Malana. Overjoyed with excitement, I turned yet another blind eye to the idea Terry was running behind my back and feeding her lies that soured not only Marlon's but my relationship with her, too. Terry made jokes and teased her about the news, and still I rationalized it away, thinking it couldn't be jealousy.

"Get in where you fit in!" Terry announced with a snarky tone upon my late arrival to the hotel, where he, some friends and family, including Rochelle and her crew of mean girls, cackled at every word he said.

I shot him an "if looks could kill" glare before he busted out laughing similarly, as if pretending the truth was a joke, but I knew I didn't fit in. At least, I didn't fit in anymore, I came to realize. I surveyed the room, astounded at all our new friends: Paul, Lisa B's husband; Lonnie; Damon; the young girls Rochelle had brought along for the free ride, who tried their best to keep up with my style; Damon's cousin Jessica, my now-close friend, who was seeing Troy, another new guy Tee let join in; and, of course, Eric.

Eric had firmly planted himself in Terry's world by this point and carried much sway over his decisions. He also wasn't shy about his womanizing and voiced his hatred for snitches incessantly. This drew much concern from me, as I felt he advocated for Tee to cheat on me, but even worse, Eric could bring him down. I just didn't believe any man who talked as much as him could be trustworthy. As his influence on Terry grew, my voice was drowned out by all the others, and I just *did not fit in* anymore.

The drugs, alcohol, and partying became more frequent. All of this only pushed the relationship into further disrepair. Terry was beginning to get sloppy and too comfortable, even though it was clear that the Feds were honing in.

Even with our best interest at heart, Terry was reluctant to see clearly. Without his support, I watched his back—not only from the law, but from those closest to us. On one occasion while watching Paul from another room, I witnessed what he routinely did, which was to drop off stacks of money. As he left some of the wads of cash on the bed, in the same motion, he purposely dropped several of them next to the bed and hid them underneath the mattress, with the intention of retrieving them later, because he knew Terry would hardly notice or even care.

I waited until he left the room and reached under the mattress and retrieved the money without saying a word. I chuckled as I thought about him coming back to find that the wads of cash had vanished, along with whatever plans he had for spending what wasn't his. I went beyond that and warned him many times not to do it again—to my own detriment. One instance over a wiretap implicated my knowledge of his dealings.

"Where you at?" I curiously asked Terry during a casual conversation over the cell phone.

"On the highway, bey, why?" he responded, as if confused.

"Roll the window down and throw that phone out," I said sternly.

He was in a good reception area and the service did not go in and out, like a standard connection issue. However, the consistent static noise in the background raised my suspicion. My inclination was to direct him to get rid of what might have been a hot phone. This was an obvious clue that our conversation was not private—and besides this one, many other calls Terry made weren't, either.

Still, I was concerned our every move was being tracked—via the cell phone Tee refused to throw away—by Agent Sarkozy, of the IRS, who was constantly on our tail, probably following the money. I recognized him in different places, even outside a Dior store in Hawaii. Only reluctantly did Tee start to believe me. Fake telephone engineers climbing poles, where there were no cables; people getting pulled over after leaving our Mulholland home— I could feel the noose tightening . . . while still shaking off any concerns that I was in trouble.

The only problem, as far as I could see, was me having agreed to sign for the house. This was the hole that had tormented me many nights and kept me from sleeping. It was just as the psychiatrist had pondered, asking me if I thought it was the direction my life was taking. It would become clearer that it wasn't the direction I thought my life was taking, but indeed a fact I was diving headfirst into my own demise.

* * *

# SECRET LOVER

In January 2005, during Terry's thirty-fifth birthday, we threw him an extravagant party, featuring Frankie Beverly and Maze, which contributed to being the final nail in the coffin—not only for Terry and Demetrius's relationship, but the DEA and FBI watched in close range. Agents attended the festivities disguised as the hotel staff's catering service and other guests, until the party was abruptly side railed by a brawl between Wayne and Eric. It started with Eric throwing the first punch, knocking Wayne's watch off his wrist. Everyone rushed in to take sides.

Security escorted us out of the ballroom and up to our hotel suite, where management requested to know who the VIP guest was, which we declined to answer. That's when the hotel manager politely asked us all to check out.

That evening, we would check into several suites at the Bellagio. A meeting was quickly held that included Meech, on the other end of the phone. The brothers decided their partnership and the family business could no longer operate in the same fashion; so the decision was made to split operations in half and each one would go his separate way. Meech would retain the name BMF, and Terry and his new crew, co-led by Eric, would take on a more understated presence; therefore, he used the numerals 263 to decipher between the two factions. Terry believed the name brought much attention and, at this point, was too hot, but it was already too late to have made these changes.

Following a trip to Miami that summer, Eric would be pulled over for what at first appeared to be a routine stop. Minutes later, he was pulled out of the car for suspected drunk driving. The police proceeded to search the car and came upon a concealed weapon. Eric was then arrested for being in possession of unregistered weapons and DUI. During detainment, he would begin helping the DEA and IRS to make a connection between the money and drugs.

Now with Eric in custody, the Feds connected the seizure of jewelry from Terry's traffic stop. Through the wiretaps where

Terry could be heard instructing Damon to claim the jewelry, and using Eric's testimony, they were able to prove that Jacob would help provide false documentation backing it up. This became the direct link the DEA needed to secure search warrants and begin going after us.

"You near a fax machine?" Ace would ask during a brief call. Ace was a broker who sold us many high-end cars, including my Aston Martin.

I'd quickly get dressed and hightail it down Beverly Glen to the nearest FedEx to receive sealed government documents of Eric's testimony after being detained in a car still owned by Ace's company, as far as paperwork went. Since according to law, he was the rightful owner of the car, he received a copy of the legal documents that would surely incriminate Ace himself, along with the rest of us.

My body trembled as I watched the fax machine spit out page after page of what was surely the undoing of Terry and me. I quickly paid the cashier and rushed back to the car and began peeling away at the pages. Name after name, and the deeds and title ownerships to homes, ended up in the documents—with my name throughout it as well. The evidence was damning, to say the least, and I knew for certain—without a doubt—Terry would have to listen to me now.

"Bitch! You're a hater! You don't know anything!" Terry screamed across the phone after I, too, instructed him to find a FedEx so I could, once again unwittingly, commit wire fraud when sending my last option to convince him that his friend had turned into a federal witness—and time was running out.

The truth hurts and inevitably Terry was headed to jail; so in some sense, I understood his lashing out wasn't personal. Lacking the ability to apologize, while also swallowing such a hard pill that he would spend the next decade in prison, was hard to bear. So I forgave him and planned to prepare for what was to come.

Our fighting would get worse as my drug and alcohol intake intensified. Shots of tequila were chased with Dom Perignon by the bottle. While the Feds closed in, the alcohol would urge me to end it, or even convinced me enough that I could drive the passenger side of my Aston Martin into a wall and kill him. While he survived from my deranged speeding and attempt at murder, the rearview mirror and side panel needed to be replaced. I lied to my kids the next day that I had sideswiped the garage as I returned the night before. Regardless, it didn't matter, as we both could see the writing on the wall.

"I'm the only one that's gone do this twenty, that's why," Terry remarked one evening.

"Don't say that!" I demanded in clear denial.

A week before Tee's capture at his St. Louis home, Meech had been busted at a rented million-dollar mansion, just outside of Dallas. Figuring my place was about to be raided, I got rid of certain items. What I didn't expect was to get arrested.

When the day arrived, Agent Sarkozy called my phone, and as soon as I opened the door, they snatched me, spun me around, put me in cuffs, and read me my rights. It was like a whirlwind.

*This can't be happening. I didn't sell no drugs,* I kept telling myself.

Countless armed agents swarmed the house and began to search. "Corey, Jason, it's the police. Just come out!" I yelled, hoping they could hear me.

While the Feds ripped apart my house, I zoned out. All I knew was my middle son, Jason, had a gun; if he thought we were being robbed, this could turn tragic. Unable to get to him or to Corey, I was scared out of my mind. *These are my babies, what are y'all gonna do to them?*

There was no violence. But the day after I was indicted, my bank account and credit cards were frozen. I then found out Tee had taken the money we'd stashed in a wall safe—and that the people he'd trusted had cleaned out all of our other homes.

# BLACK MAFIA QUEEN

The only thing left was my Benz, which Paul stole right from in front of our Mulholland estate while I was recovering from a mastectomy, originally scheduled for the day of my arrest. By October 2005, 635 kilos and $14,000,000 had been seized, while arrests were made of forty-seven BMF members, including Meech, Tee, and me.

Surviving on some money that no one else knew about, I was living in an altered reality of boozing and drugging. Wiretaps of Tee's phone confirmed the names of the women he'd been cheating with; hearing that really hurt. Come to find out it wasn't just one woman, but it was the least expected of them all that cut deep, and with Marlon also going to prison, the damage was irreparable when I found out Terry was also sneaking around with Rochelle—the mother to my first grandchild, the girl who had become like a daughter to me, was taunting me straight to my face.

Many times, I had suspected something fishy was going on between her and Tee, but I never had any proof of it. It all now lay in front of me, downloaded to several DVDs for me to hear myself, provided by the federal government as part of its transparency involving the investigation. Hours upon hours of Terry and Rochelle flirting; planning secret rendezvous; and betraying both of our trust; secretly allowing Rochelle to hear conversations with Marlon, where they discussed other women, divulging his whereabouts; and Tee tirelessly disparaging me, and Eric, finally fed up from hearing it, would dare him to just leave me if he was so unhappy.

*How could I have been so blind?* I thought. Sick, in despair, and distraught that I had failed my eldest son, it was hard to focus on any one thing. Although my attorney told me to prepare myself for prison, I couldn't wrap my head around how I'd adjust to that—while living with the constant mental anguish of not knowing which would be my last day of freedom. Depressed, unable to really eat or sleep, I relied on over-the-counter medication as my only coping mechanism.

# SECRET LOVER

* * *

To think I could have been out. I could've taken the small in comparison to what I would have been leaving, but I'd still have a substantial amount of cash, which I had put away for a rainy day, as they say. I was even urged on by some of my friends and confidants.

"Hey, Toni. I got this property I want you to see. Can you meet me?" Stacy inquired one morning. Stacy was an event planner from Los Angeles; we commissioned her for most of our parties, including Terry's Vegas birthday extravaganza. She had been dating an old male friend of ours, and he originally introduced her to us. She had become a close friend.

"Come on, we're going to meet Stacy," I said to Corey.

Taking Corey along for the ride, we ventured through the hills to a modest home in a cul-de-sac in Tarzana, California. It was an older home, with a beautiful entranceway that opened up to a staircase and several other landings. Corey, ever the enthusiast, zipped off to take his own tour of the home, while Stacy and I stayed behind, taking a slower pace.

"Isn't it beautiful? It just needs a little work," Stacy remarked.

Curious as to why she had brought me here, and the intentions behind it, I was at a loss for words, unsure of exactly what to say.

"Well, me and Lawrence, we're going to move in, but with his situation, I don't need the space, but its mine, free and clear."

"I'm not looking for a home," I stated blankly.

"I know, I know. But, Toni, don't you think you should get out of this?"

I bristled at the question, unsure of what she was getting at, nor had it dawned on me that maybe she knew more than she was saying.

"I just want you to be happy. You and Corey can move here and leave all that behind."

"Leave *what* behind?" I shouted back.

Stacy's eyes began to water just as Corey made his way back

**121**

down. "You ready." Clearly unimpressed, Corey was ready to go. I quickly handed over the car key and motioned for him to wait in the car.

"Toni, I care about you. I don't want you going through this."

I stood there, silently trying to figure out what to say without leading on that I knew the curtains were beginning to close on me and Terry.

Stacy began to weep. "I love you and Corey. I don't want anything to happen to you guys. You can just move here."

"Everything's okay, girl. I know me and Tee go through it, but I love him. I'm not ready to give up on us."

Stacy stared back at me with a blank face. She either didn't hear what I said or was convinced I was delusional, but she couldn't say it. She then held her arms open for an embrace, and we hugged for what seemed like an eternity as she cried on my shoulder.

"Everything's going to be okay." I attempted to console her, even though everything wasn't okay. Her boyfriend had already been indicted on a separate case, and it wouldn't be long before Terry and I would join him.

As I drove away with an uneasy feeling in my spirit, it wouldn't dawn on me until later that Stacy had already been approached by the FBI because of her dealings with us. After Terry's birthday and many attempts to collect the photos taken during the event, Stacy had put me off several times with silly excuses and apologizing for the delay. It later came to my knowledge that the DEA had confiscated many of the raw images from the photographer to gather more information about Terry and our associates. It explained, as well, how the uninvited guests and undercover staff members came to attend Terry's birthday bash.

Ever since Marlon's arrest, the bottom had fallen out of my world. I was now just biding my time, waiting to *do* time, yet the judge kept granting me extensions while federal crimes were laid at the feet of more and more BMF members: 150 of them by 2007.

# SECRET LOVER

Having walked away from the Mulholland home a year after my indictment, I now bought a modest place in Playa Vista, rented it out, and moved into my youngest son Corey's two-bedroom Northridge apartment.

While the federal government alleged BMF had generated over $270,000,000 in revenue, all of us were stripped of our assets. So much for Meech's attempt to legitimize the organization via his hip-hop music label, BMF Entertainment, and his lifestyle magazine, *The Juice*. The game was up. In September 2008, the Flenory brothers each received thirty-year sentences for heading a drug-trafficking organization. My sentence for money laundering was fifty-seven months.

# Chapter 15

# Fear of the Unknown

*Fall 2008*

Cue to the three-day going-away party before I turned my-self in.

I stood in the mirror just staring, unsure of who the reflection gazing back at me was. With knots in my stomach, my thoughts raced, unable to stick to one single idea. Deep down, I knew it was fear—fear of the unknown—and of what was to come. I could only prepare my boys so much before this day, and for the first time in their lives, I would have to leave them to fend for themselves. I overcompensated. Yeah, they didn't grow up with a step-father, or a bio father, like I had, so I made up for it a lot, or at least tried to. I didn't make the best choices in that area, and I fucked up many times. *But I'm all they have,* I thought as I scanned the room. *Time is running out on me. I'm never on time for shit and I always push my limits.*

It was time to change out of the dress from the night before and head out. Already having done my research online, and from the advice of friends and family, I knew what to expect when I arrived at the prison. I certainly knew to come in something comfortable, warm, and easy to change out of. Even still, I couldn't pull it together. I must've changed a dozen times, as if I were heading off to a date or a meeting, with the objective of impressing someone.

Pausing, I spun the tricolored ring around on my finger. It was a simple piece compared to all of the other jewelry I owned. It was my favorite—a simple Cartier band comprised of three types of gold. Still not fully dressed, I fumbled with it as I made sure to put away the rest of my belongings and tried to recall if I was forgetting anything: Did I forget to mention anything to my boys? Did I remind Corey to look after the mortgage payments? As I was wrestling with these questions, I heard a knock at the door.

"Mom, what's that on your back?" Corey asked, clearly alarmed to see something on my exposed skin.

Still not wearing a blouse, my back was turned to him when he entered the doorway to check on me. "What, what is it?" I asked in a panic. I turned my back toward the mirror and tried to peer over my shoulder to see what he was talking about. *What the hell did I do last night?* I thought. In my drunken stupor, could I have gone off and gotten a tattoo like a renegade teen would?

"Right here!" he exclaimed, touching just between my shoulder blades. "It looks like wings," he calmly remarked.

I didn't see anything, but that was it. It was a sign to me that God was letting me know my angels were there to protect me and I would be fine on this next journey. I pulled the ring off my finger and placed it with my other belongings in a plastic ziplock bag, grabbed my blouse from the bed, and put on some tennis shoes. "Let's go, I'm ready."

On day two at Victorville Federal Prison Camp, I was sent to the rock pile and ordered by a woman guard, who made the most of every opportunity, to strip. Whenever she saw me in a hallway, she'd pull me into a room and tell me to undress. When I eventually reported this to the unit manager, he told me, "You can either put up with it or make things worse for yourself." I had to put up with it—and would continue to do so during my whole stay.

It made no sense to move boulders no more than ten feet and I refused to do it, even though Maria, my Mexican bunkmate, warned, "They'll put you in the hole." In the end, she moved the rocks for me—and I realized I had a true friend.

Federal prison in California is very segregated: Black people hang with each other; Caucasians and Hispanics do the same. But I was never that kind of person. I could get along with anybody and had no interest in cliquing up. Still, I was really kind of private. Most of the girls would try to figure me out; and although I'd talk to a few of them, it would only be for long enough not to make trouble. I never told any of them what I'd done to end up behind bars.

As I mentioned earlier in the book, everyone predicted I'd be working in the warehouse, which was the worst job in the compound. My counselor confirmed it when I visited his office, and my heart sank. I admit, I felt so sorry for myself; I was such a loser . . . until, as I was about to walk out the door, I heard him say, "Miss Welch, you're going to work in the chapel."

*Whoa, okay.* I really couldn't get that encounter out of my head. For days, I wasn't quite sure what that meant for the journey ahead, but it gave me a slight glimpse of hope and reassurance that God hadn't completely abandoned me. In fact, it was quite the opposite. I had been placed in a position to study and finally think straight. My mind was becoming clearer and less convoluted, improving from the years of abuse that my own boozing and my sheer avoidance of reality brought on. I also was now freed from the manipulation of the man I once trusted and believed was my best friend.

Up until then, I'd never realized how many religions there are. Now I was reading all about them—and talking with the psychologist who worked next door to the chapel.

# FEAR OF THE UNKNOWN

"You need to think about why you're so angry and why you're in this situation," he said after hearing my woe-is-me bitching.

So I thought about it while I worked in that chapel every day, from eight o'clock in the morning until four-thirty in the afternoon: praying, reading, and then praying and reading again, in a repetitive cycle in the hope that something would click. *It just had to,* I thought. *I mean, how the hell else did I wind up here?* God, *answer me!* Only one person could work in the chapel; how amazing that it was me who was assigned the job. From there, I'd sweep my way down to the psychologist's office. "Let me buff your floors and empty your trash," I offered.

This enabled me to see him more and keep talking—about the choices I'd made, all the way down the line, as well as how much and how long I'd been manipulating and getting away with shit. Still sad, still bitter, I wasn't yet ready to admit the role I'd played in my own downfall. In talking to some of the other inmates, I also realized my sentence was peanuts compared to theirs—and they couldn't even touch the kind of life I'd led.

Fuck, a quarter-million-dollar car, hundreds of thousands of dollars in clothes and bags, multiple homes across the country, and countless stamps in my passport—half of the women incarcerated with me had never left their block, let alone the state. Some of their parents were too elderly to even drive to visit, or their kids were too young to come on their own—if they even knew where they were. I was beyond blessed, despite my circumstances. It could've been much worse. This was something I was reminded of constantly.

The road to rehabilitation would be rough, but there would have been no chance of fixing myself, had I been working in the warehouse.

# Chapter 16

# The Smell of Roses

SITTING IN THE CHURCH LIBRARY, READING ALL KINDS OF BOOKS—religious, law, and self-help—I began educating myself. Sitting in the chapel, I'd pray for guidance. Still bitter, blaming the world, I only felt guilty about leaving my sons. I could talk to Corey and Jason, but not to Marlon. Even if he wrote from jail, his letters would have to go through Corey to get to me. So I just kept bouncing between anger and guilt.

"Make sure to get change before you get here," I instructed Corey, once he picked up my free collect call. It was our first visit since I had turned myself in and I wasn't sure he remembered from the last visit with his father, years prior, that the vending machines in the visitation room only took quarters. It was early Saturday morning, and he still sounded groggy. In excitement of his arrival, I woke up and went to use the phones as soon as it was allowed.

"I know. I remember, Mom." Halfway annoyed, he didn't need constant reminding; even though I was away, I felt my baby still needed me, but it began to feel that the roles were becoming reversed. Now I clearly needed him to handle anything I couldn't from inside.

"Okay, I'm heading out!" he said.

# THE SMELL OF ROSES

"The visit starts at eight in the morning. Don't be late, please!" I stressed once more.

"I won't," he assured me.

A lot had fallen on Corey at that time. Juggling school, an internship at Universal Music, paying bills, and maintaining his own social life was a lot to put on such a young man. It was specially hard for someone who had never been on his own and now had to fend for himself. I was thankful he made so much time to drive and see me. I thought it must be selfish of me to call and imply that I didn't trust he would remember to stop and get at least $20 in change or arrive on time—just so I could spend as much time as I could with him.

I rushed to shower and pull out my freshly creased and tailored inmate garments. Even if I couldn't wear the latest collection from Gucci, I still made sure my uniform looked the best it could. Some of the other inmates just threw on whatever was clean and didn't care how it fit their frame, but I insisted on learning how to sew and tailored my clothes so I could look as presentable as possible for when my family came to visit.

It didn't stop there. Reading the magazines Corey and others ordered for me, I learned at-home remedies for exfoliating my skin and moisturizing. Using contraband lifted from the kitchen and products bought from the commissary, I would mix and experiment with eggs, yeast, and other ointments to clear blemishes and dry out outbreaks caused by the heavy preservative meals served in the kitchen, and the snacks and junk food from the vending machines during visits. I was clearly learning how to take care of myself without all the hired help, expensive clothes, and high-priced products sold in department stores.

As Corey arrived and was guided into the small visiting room, along with several families, I waited for my name to be called. As soon as I heard, "Welch, report to the visitation room," I ran out of the dorm room.

# BLACK MAFIA QUEEN

"Have a good visit!" Maria yelled after me.

Crossing over the courtyard into a smaller room, I stopped where the same female guard did a routine strip search before I started my visit. I undressed and she looked me over before commanding I bend over so she could get a good glance of my cavities. *Clear!* She waited for me to replace my clothes, then crossed over to another heavy iron door and unlocked it with a single key from her large set of keys, which were connected to her waist.

"That's the bitch that's always making me strip," I whispered to Corey after rushing over to give him a huge hug before sitting at the table in a corner with him. He tried to steal a glance, unsure if she was looking our way as she hid her eyes behind a hideous pair of dark shades. "She probably just likes seeing my coochie," I quipped. "A lot of the female guards and other inmates are like that here," I continued.

Astounded, Corey asked, "Is it like they say?"

"No, people don't just get raped. These girls will say prison made them lesbian, but that's just an excuse. They were like that before they came in," I elaborated further. "Some of them don't even want to leave because they're in love. They will even fight you if they think you're talking to someone they like. Couldn't be me," I finished.

I went on to explain to Corey that some of the girls gave me a hard time, but I stood my ground. One tried to stop me from using the phone, until I made it clear I'd knock her ass out with it.

"Oh, you ain't playing," she said, trying to laugh it off.

After that, we were cool; she didn't mess with me. Others would come on to me, testing to see if I was bi or gay. That didn't fly, either. When in 2010, Mara Shalhoup's book about the BMF was published, everybody started talking about it—and whispering about me because my name appeared throughout. The gossip was going around and finally someone approached me.

"Oh, so you Ms. BMF? Bitch, we thought you was selling real estate, not a fucking drug queen."

**130**

# THE SMELL OF ROSES

After that, there was a different level of respect from the inmates, not that I courted it. They just went out of their way to speak with me and invite me into their different circles. But I wasn't there for long; after eighteen months in Victorville, I was transferred to the low-security Federal Correctional Institution in Dublin, California. An outdoor facility connected to an army base, it housed the inmates in army trailers and houses. Now I'd get to see trees, flowers, and cars passing by—just like the camp they showed me in the video after my sentencing, or so I thought.

"I used to wonder why people said, 'Stop and smell the roses,'" I mused with Corey during one of his visits. "Now I fucking get it!" We both laughed. "I am so tired of these women, the dumb shit, and being stuck here. After all that time in the desert with no view, I finally get it."

When I finally got to go outside, I could see, stop, and smell the roses. At last, I could appreciate just being outside and seeing some greenery. What I eventually came to realize was that I'd always been an enabler for—and co-dependent with—all those that I wanted love from: my mom, my friends, my boyfriends, my kids. Growing up not knowing what love was, I'd convinced myself that what I did for a man somehow equaled him giving me love. Everything in my life was a deal, not just the drugs.

Thanks to my counselor, I was entered into a drug program, despite not really qualifying for it. Another reason to count my blessings. "Stop blaming everybody else," I was told. "You're a strong woman; you started this journey long ago. Start working on yourself."

Talking with my psychologist and the chaplain were my refuge from the guard who was always harassing me. She wouldn't say anything when they were around. And I'd stay near them every day until call time.

On the first day in Dublin, I was locked inside the women's high-security prison across the street. And I panicked. "Y'all need to call my family. I'm in the wrong spot. This has got to be a mistake," I complained.

As it turned out, it had been a mistake. After thirty-six hours of mental torture, I was fished out of this dungeon and walked back across the street. Relief rushed over my body as I was escorted out of the small bare cage, which I feared would be my new home for the next few months. It was in this moment that I could smell the roses for the first time as I took in the fresh Northern California air. Although I wasn't completely free, at least I wasn't caged away in a high-security facility, with little access to the outside air, nor were there heavy metal doors locked from the outside. Nor did I have to worry about the threat of a warehouse job anymore or the trivial task of moving rocks from one spot to another.

Then while in the camp yard, taking in the surroundings, I saw a guard size me up. *Here we go again,* I thought.

"Come here," he said. "Your first day? Who's your counselor?"

"Ms. Teethen."

"You're a good-looking woman. She's gonna give you a hard time," the guard said to me.

I felt a lump in my stomach as the words left his mouth. Once again, I would need to watch my back and stay clear of the one person who held my freedom in their hands. *How does this shit happen?* I asked myself.

My new counselor was nasty right from the start. Ms. Teethen was an older Caucasian woman, with snow-white hair, whose chunky face always seemed to have an evil sneer. When I approached her to let her know I didn't have an ID number to use the phone, she replied, "I'll give it to you when I *want* to give it to you."

It was a Thursday. She was off the next three days, so I didn't have a chance to call my family and tell them, "Hey, I made it to the low-security outdoor prison. Once I complete the drug program, I can come home."

During this time, my biological father's health began to fail after being diagnosed with dementia, and soon it would be the time to say goodbye. I tried to call as much as I could, but not being allowed to use the phone, I felt my fear skyrocket. What if I wasn't able to speak with him in time? His memory was fading, and he was hardly able to speak sometimes when I called, so it already was tough on me, but not being able to say goodbye was one of my biggest fears.

Instead of helping me get through the rest of my term, Ms. Teethen was making it hell for me. For no apparent reason, I wasn't given phone privileges. "You're not gonna make it through the drug program," she said. "I'm gonna do everything in my power to get you kicked off it.

"I don't give a fuck about your dead daddy or whoever," she continued. "I'm not giving you a temporary release or any other privileges because some stupid family member of yours decided to keel over."

I felt my eyes glaze over as I clenched my jaw tight enough to crush my teeth. It took the strength of six ancestors, God, and the thought of the two young men I left at home who were waiting, and needed their mother, for me to control the growing rage inside me.

"You really think I care yo daddy died?" she asked coldly.

Frozen, I just stared back, unable to mumble a single syllable that wouldn't be harmful. In stark contrast to the women with whom you're serving time, the ladies on the other side of the fence had absolutely nothing in common with us criminals, other than we found ourselves unfortunately colliding.

"Do you have something to add?" Ms. Teethen glared.

"No, ma'am." This wasn't like eating just a slice of humble pie. This was equivalent to the entire pie being shoved down my throat while I was waterboarded. In that moment, I felt I could sink no lower.

What in my profile and psych analysis made her want to be so mean? When my biological dad passed away in April 2011, old

Teethen called me into her office and said, "Bitch, you can forget about going to the funeral. I don't give a fuck about you, your momma, your daddy, or your motherfucking kids. You ain't going nowhere. Fuck you. Now get outta here."

There was no one else I could go to and ask, "Can you assign me to somebody else?"

On many days when they would call mail, I'd rush over to see a letter forwarded by Corey from Marlon. I'd eagerly tear the envelope open and read his handwritten words and imagine his voice. I found refuge in his letters many days when I felt hopeless, and guilt-ridden—especially as the thought of my father slowly drifting away in his bed tormented me. How did I put myself in this position, completely restricted from comforting my father and eldest son? At least, I found solace in his letters as he reassured me that he was doing fine and was in great spirits. He encouraged me by saying that if he could get through this, then so could I. Whether anyone stood up for me or not, I would not let this time break or trigger me into doing something regrettable that could incite Ms. Teethen into taking my time or adding more than originally sentenced. Those types tend to stick together.

I remembered being on my knees in the chapel every day, praying I'd get into the drug program. Although I was devastated after initially being denied, a friend named Jill, serving a ten-year sentence, dropped out at the last minute just so I could get in and go home early. My counselor couldn't stop it because the drug program was a separate entity, and she had nothing to do with it. Once more, I was blessed.

One day, someone running the program told me, "She's doing everything she can, even going to the warden to get you kicked out. So long as you don't do anything she can nail you with, we've got your back. Just be careful and stay away from her."

"She's fucking him." Shirley nodded her head toward one of the guards on duty. She was conversing in between biting into her burger as we sat outside. The guard was a burly Black man with a clean face. He smiled and made small talk with some of the other inmates as he walked toward another administrative building. He wasn't my type, but he clearly looked like the kind of man who would be sleeping with Teethen or whoever else was desperate enough to give him some.

"Hmm, no wonder," I mumbled just as he looked over at us. Not wanting to stir trouble, I kept my head down just long enough for him to go away. Lest he find an interest in me, or someone told my counselor that I was attempting to talk to him, either could cause us both undue trouble. I had to do my best not to court his or any of the other male guards' attention while here, especially his. If I knew anything, the best way to get on a woman's bad side, or get time added, was to be seen having an unsavory conversation with a staff member of the Federal Bureau of Prisons. To hell if I would allow that to be the case.

To avoid trouble, I ate in my room, instead of the dining hall, on the days my counselor was at work. That woman looked like the devil. No way was I going to let that bitch break me. Instead, over time, jail actually ended up building my spirit. Stronger at my emotional core, I gradually became more comfortable with who I am and less reliant on the approval of others.

With my father's passing, I became laser focused on building myself up and figuring out what I wanted to do with my life post incarceration. My mother and stepfather were still alive and able-bodied; and when Corey visited, they would sometimes come along as well. My stepfather still ran and operated the car service we started decades before, and while he was supportive, he stayed on the run and was eager to get back to Detroit.

My mother came, as much as possible, and we would make plans in between playing Scrabble and Uno. She was my rock, my biggest supporter, and at times my harshest critic, but it was all in wanting the best for me. Now sitting in prison, I began to discover the best for me wasn't in a man, or in anyone else, but within myself.

"I don't know what he spends it on. He just spends all our little money," my mom would relay to me one day about Emerson's spending habits. They both pulled in a sizable pension, plus his postretirement business seemed to make a sizable income, too, but still my mother complained, and all I could do was listen behind bars. I wasn't able to help or be there in the way I used to be.

Who was I now without being able to pull wads of cash out of my pocketbook or write a check on the spot when she needed? That was something I had to face, and it became clear that after all the support and energy I put into men, I should have focused a lot of that on myself. It wasn't just me who suffered from this indelible trait, but the other countless women I was serving time with also suffered for caring and loving someone else above themselves.

Despite my efforts to improve myself, some habits die hard. Not long after getting settled in at Dublin, I was tasked with being shipped over to the army base to work. There I noticed we had complete autonomy to do as we pleased. We could talk to the staff and carry on relationships right under the BOP's nose, as long as we kept our mouths shut and didn't become pregnant. The prison staff had no idea what went on just across the way. We weren't monitored or restricted when on the base. It was the closest thing to being free.

Always scheming, I figured out how to sell cigarettes supplied by army guys on the base. "Hey, come here!" I gestured for Jill and Cassie to come over to me as we finished mopping the dining hall one evening. "I got an idea." As my friends Jill and Cassie were serving more time than me, and had less money, I persuaded them to smuggle the cigarettes into the prison. "Now, when we get back, just act like you don't like me," I continued.

# THE SMELL OF ROSES

"We don't want them to get onto us. So, if we pretend to not be friends, they'll never suspect it's us."

Even though they were already planning on having relationships with the army men, I convinced some of the sex-starved girls not to just fuck the men for nothing, but to get them to agree to do favors in exchange for extras: Burger King, KFC, other fast-food meals . . .

"Y'all doubling up with money, cigarettes, and a bit on the side," I emphasized. Everyone would be happy.

We all swore ourselves to secrecy, since it was our freedom on the line, after all—not to mention a minor lucrative business that helped the women out and provided us with some bonus extras that made the time just a bit easier to deal with. If we got caught, however, that would spell the end of the drug program for me and also lead to my good time being revoked.

From time to time, we would even get alcohol. If not, we would take yeast from the kitchen pantry and concoct our own moonshine in buckets, which we would let sit and oxidize over several days. We'd enjoy it on the weekends, when less staff members were on campus. We threw parties, like we were at home, for someone's birthday, or anyone going home after reaching the end of their sentence.

I'd also continued to explore my creative side after journaling my experiences every day, at the suggestion of Sam Woods. At first, I was reluctant. *What grown-ass woman has a diary?* I thought. However, with more time on my hands, and little to do after reading all the magazines I received in the mail, I began to write down my thoughts, finding a self-awareness I had never felt before. It was even more therapeutic than wasting all that money on a psychiatrist. It opened me up to writing poems, which Corey would also help with on his visits.

Trying to find some clarity, I would send them to Corey to forward to Marlon and Terry as well. This is about the time when I started to take accountability for my own deeds. Marlon joined in helping to write insightful poems, which we believed could become records, and Terry responded with his own poetry, asking for forgiveness.

"Remember when you told me about those toilets?" Terry sheepishly asked when he was awaiting his case to proceed.

"Yes," I answered back.

"Now I understand what you meant. I can't believe I thought that shit was fly."

During renovations to the White House in Atlanta, Terry had excitedly guided me to a bathroom that was newly finished with a stainless-steel toilet and sink.

*Why would you do that?* I thought. The first thing that came to my mind were the toilets you see in jail cells.

Terry, who had never been incarcerated for as much as a speeding ticket, did not see his foibles. To me, it looked like a prison stall! It certainly didn't give the perception of class or style in the least.

"You will regret it," I stated coyly, which he didn't take well.

Terry called me a "hater" for months after that, and even invoked my son Corey to join in and agree with him from time to time. But now he understood what I had meant; and unfortunately for me, I realized it was clearly an omen for us both.

While I idly sat back thinking his actions and opinion had no effect on where I was headed, the stainless-steel toilet was a bleak representation that eventually both our lives were going to be pulled down the drain by the very home where it was installed.

Prison came with its own set of rules. Never leave the sink wet, tidy your bunk before leaving, and get comfortable with having to use the toilet around other women—not to mention showering and brushing your teeth while someone took a dump just a few stalls down. This was all new to me and I grew accustomed to having to clean up after grown-ass women who left the toilet nasty and left their personal items in the shower.

It was surely no way to live and a constant reminder of that moment in Atlanta, but it fueled my drive to never return once I was released.

When the drug counselor made me camp leader and I refused, he threatened me by saying, "If you don't do it, we'll take your time."

They had to force me to open up, talk about my life, and cry. I was clammed up like a vault, but when I became camp leader, I had to counsel women. What I later realized was that the counseling wasn't for them, it was for me, because now I had to share my story.

It's true what they say, you don't know how many people you help by living your truth. I could have never imagined the effect I would have on the other women. Until then, I kept to myself, especially in regard to my past. I was surrounded by so many young girls and they had never had an older woman to look to for guidance, or to serve as a positive mother figure for them.

I saw myself in a lot of their journeys, and I could relate to many of the mistakes they made. I realized how at our core we were all searching for love in the wrong places, people, and material items. It became clear as I retold my story, over and over again, how I hadn't actually found true love for myself.

Some of the women who didn't like me began to come around and started to share their own testimonies about insecurities, infidelity, and shame. "I don't like you or your creased pants," a girl named Courtney told me one afternoon on the track. Courtney was a Black girl in her thirties who was dealing with a lot of repressed anger. Abandoned by her mother at a young age, she had never met her father and was in and out of orphanages until she became of age. Then she moved from motel to motel, turning tricks and doing whatever drug her deadbeat boyfriend peddled to her.

I chuckled. Something as simple as wanting to crease my clothes and valuing my appearance bothered her to the core. "That's okay, you gone love me by the time I leave," I retorted humorously. I learned not to take negative comments or petty jealousies seriously. It was a far cry from who I used to be, and what I would have done to make her change her mind.

Every day throughout the program, I was convinced Ms. Teethen would find something to hang on me. I was scared I wouldn't make it home. Sure, the drug program counselors had my back, but I still felt nervous. Even when my name was finally called to leave, I couldn't believe it, and I was almost hyperventilating because I had such a fear of her.

Courtney rushed over to me with tears running down her face. "I love you, bitch!" she bellowed.

I began to cry, too, as many of the women came to wish me goodbye and good luck on the outside. It was an overwhelming feeling. I had come to know and love many of these women as well. We shared so much with each other. Some of the women's sons became friends with Corey on the outside. We cried and laughed about the past, the present, our daily struggles, and shared our dreams for the future. The day had finally arrived for me to begin to pursue those dreams and to work for a brighter future than I ever imagined.

It felt unreal. Already changed out of my prison uniform, and into some brand-new street clothes and Christian Louboutin heels Corey had mailed me weeks prior in preparation for my release, I was about to step out a brand-spanking-new woman. There would be no more watching over my shoulder for Teethen or even the Feds. The many sleepless nights spent wondering if today would be the day it would all come crashing down were now over.

Yet, still to the very end, I held my breath waiting on someone to grab or stop me in my tracks and say there had been a mistake, but it was just doubt playing tricks with my head. All of these thoughts and feelings were quickly dispelled with every step I took farther away, until finally the camp disappeared in the rear-view mirror of the cab that took me to the airport, with strict orders to report to the halfway house upon arrival in Los Angeles.

Released in June of 2011, I was required to stay at a halfway house in Silver Lake, California, until the first day of 2012. Then I returned home . . . to nothing.

# Chapter 17
# Homeless

*2007 to January 1, 2012*

"THE IRS PUT A LIEN ON YOUR HOME," LESLIE INFORMED ME after our house had been raided and I was indicted and then released. Leslie was our Realtor in Los Angeles. She helped sell some of our properties and walked me through the quick deed process of the Atlanta home. Having dealt with her own dark past and dealings with the Feds herself decades before, she helped walk me through the process of walking away from my Bel-Air home.

The government had placed a forfeiture on the estate, and I'd be forced to give up all claims to it. In my haste to find a new place to live until Corey graduated, and with the intent of renting it out until I returned home, I purchased a quaint townhome in Playa Vista, a small community within Marina del Rey, California, much to the chagrin of the lead prosecutor.

"Your Honor, Ms. Welch has purchased another home. I would like to make the court aware of it," stated Dawn Ison, head of the DEA's prosecution.

The judge responded with little interest to my actions beyond the indictment. "As I said before, Ms. Welch has some rights to providing herself shelter. This is not a witch hunt."

# HOMELESS

Relieved, I thought I could have gotten myself into deeper trouble, but the judge sided with my defense. I made plans to rent the place out, once I began my stint in prison, leaving Corey to handle the mortgage payments after showing him how to balance bills. Robbing Peter to pay Paul, when necessary, I felt reassured he could handle it. That was, until doubt was cast by an ill-intentioned friend of mine.

"Corey can't handle all of that on his own," Jessica said convincingly.

*Maybe it is too much for Corey,* I thought. He would already have enough on his plate balancing school, work, and tending to my many needs and assignments while behind bars. It was a lot to task a teenager, barely out of high school.

"Heather can handle it. She's been doin' real estate for years. She has her license and her own money." Heather was a close friend and business associate of Jessica's, who sold real estate and had her broker's license. She appeared legit and seemed to be doing well for herself at the time.

"I don't know," I responded reluctantly.

"That's a lot of money to leave him responsible for," Jessica finished.

Yeah, it was, I agreed. If I allowed Heather to manage the payments, she could also screen and place new renters in the place, if and when the time came. I made the mistake of trusting her and her godsister to make the payments on the million-dollar home with my mother's name attached to it. As I sat in prison, they rerouted the payments from the mortgage company into their own bank account.

"I can't be chasing her down, Toni. We're not talking right now," Jessica told me while on a visit with my mother during my incarceration.

Having tasked her with helping my mother track down Heather, and to work with her to repair the damage, she suddenly pulled the carpet from under my feet, claiming no responsibility for the woman she once spoke so highly of. My mother stayed for an elongated amount of time with Corey, attempting to meet with her and resolve the issue to no avail.

"Just forget it," I told Corey over the phone. "I don't want my mother or you getting into trouble for my fuckup. We will figure it out when I get home."

Defeated, I had just about given up hope, not only on the home I looked forward to moving back into, but on the people I thought I could trust and rely upon. Jessica's so-called godsister had run off with thousands of dollars in missed mortgage payments—and had done Lord only knows what with the money. It's no telling if Jessica had schemed from the very beginning to cheat me out of money and a home, but it was evident she didn't care now. There was little I could do while sitting in prison. I would have to let it go, along with many other things I'd learn to live without in my new journey.

With little left, Corey never moved out of his college apartment, and he'd gain yet another roommate when I was forced to move in with him and my middle son, Jason.

*Oh, I can bounce back from this,* I kept telling myself. *I've done it before; I can do it again.*

Without a college education, I couldn't get a high-paying job. So I worked as a mall concierge, just to get out of the halfway house; and then I went from one gig to another, always trying to upgrade. But the money was never enough for the kind of life I wanted to lead.

Back home, I was known as the girl who could connect people. I'd only done three years inside and folks had been sitting around, waiting. "We know you still got the connects."

Fuck, no. Prison hadn't been a walk in the park. And although I did sell a few pounds of weed for a short while, I was determined to stick this out, as hard as it might be. Still messed up and damaged, I didn't want to end up back in the slammer.

# Chapter 18
# Growing Through It

*Corey's narration*
*2008 to 2011*

Jason, his girlfriend, and I rode back from the Victorville Federal Prison Camp, somber, without uttering a word, until we arrived back at my Northridge apartment. I tried to picture in my head how the process was going and what my mom was up to in her first few hours there, but it was hard to imagine it not being a difficult experience.

I sat in the back seat, hoping she was comfortable, and that maybe by chance a mistake had been made, and she'd call and ask us to retrieve her. However, as we drew closer back to Los Angeles, reality started to sink in. It was just me and Jason left to pick up the pieces.

Life didn't stop; it was only just beginning. We pooled cash together that my mom had left us, which turned out to be a small nest egg to survive on. With the help of an older family friend named James, who showed me how to wrap and send packages of weed, we were able to manage okay. The money was good, but hardly legal; each day was another risk for us to end up on the wrong end of the law. Still, I worked to make a better life for myself and those around me.

Langston, who was a friend I met after my mother was indicted, and became a close confidant of mine, happened to come across a small sum of money: about a thousand dollars, which he gave me to "invest." It turned out to be a complete disaster at the first attempt after leaving it to my brother Jason, who seemed to have squandered it. From there, it lit a fire in me to hustle and make a way by any means.

"I got a way for us to actually make some money," I revealed to Langston with trepidation. I was not sure if I could actually pull it off. "I'll take this money and put it in with James. After the money comes back, we can get out on our own."

Feeling confident, I looked to him for confirmation. Once again, I was risking his money and proposing yet another scheme I knew could work, but I would have to get James to agree. The next day, I met James at his luxury apartment in Westwood and proposed adding to the pot.

"It'll take about a week," James remarked. It was a sure bet and a 100 percent return. So, without saying another word, I left him with an additional two grand to invest into our pot, keeping to myself that Langston and I had plans to start our own weed business.

In between taking prerequisites at California State University, Northridge, I would receive a crash course from James in how to vacuum seal and package marijuana into overnight boxes to be shipped out the next morning. Business was lucrative and it afforded me and Langston the luxury of having an extravagant lifestyle. We hit the mall, buying the latest Nikes, dined out at pricey restaurants, and dropped cash on tables at nightclubs.

I wasn't just helping my family. Somehow I managed to help keep Langston's brothers in the private school they attended, when his grandmother found herself struggling to pay their tuition. It gave me a sense of accomplishment and belonging, which I hadn't been able to feel growing up, seeing as I always kept my distance from friends who weren't a part of the family. Now that the mystique was gone and the façade began to fade, I was able to have friends from my own merit, and it felt good not to live with such a heavy burden.

The money brought distractions, as Langston decided not to go further with his basketball career or pursue a degree. My grades began to falter as well. It seemed I was always tasked with weighing the benefits of ignoring my phone buzzing in my pants pocket during my economics lecture.

*Risk the chance of getting paid today or wait until after the class is over,* I would think. *Fuck that!* Many times, I had waited, only not to get an answer afterward, and would play phone tag with the person on the other end. When the money called, I would have to check back in on my studies when it was convenient.

It felt like I was being backed into a corner when it came to choosing between my work and studies. I needed to make sure I had a steady income, to keep up with bills and my lifestyle, but I knew the way I was making it wasn't a guarantee. Plus, from what I saw with my parents, it definitely had no future. Still, school seemed to stand in the way as my supervisor at Universal Music Group began to ask me what I wanted to do next when my contract was up interning in the publishing department.

She took an interest in me, especially after I insisted on sending over a record to be cut by a singer signed to Interscope Records. My supervisor, although hesitant about it, sent it over, anyway, which went to my mentor, Shawn "Tubby" Holiday. I had previously interned for him and he helped secure me a spot there. When I learned they would cut the record, I felt like I was on cloud nine and things were finally going to move in a positive direction. Cutting the record meant the label would record it. If they felt it was strong enough, it'd possibly get placed, which would result in a check being cut, but doubt crept in as I sat at lunch one afternoon with my supervisor, who tried to get a feel of what I wanted to do next.

"I don't know. I like it here, but I think I want to pursue film," I said in between bites of my shrimp spring rolls.

"Well, you should give it some thought, because we can't place you in the same department, but we could help you get somewhere else in the company."

Deep down, I didn't think the job was a right fit for her. She didn't seem to have that same connection to music I had seen previously when I was shadowing Damon or interning for Shawn. What was clear, though, is she didn't want me around to step on her toes or possibly become competition for her job. After my time was up, I looked for industry jobs in film, with no luck, as my school schedule conflicted with every callback I received. It felt hopeless and I began to drift further into my own life of crime.

This turned out to be the straw that broke the camel's back. Disenchanted with school, and pulled by the allure of a career in music or film, I became more comfortable with taking risks for the instant gratification of getting money the fast and easy way. James became my influence, inspiring me to believe I could succeed in shipping packs of weed out as my time became less grounded in my prior responsibilities. My past goals faded as I set new ones similar to his.

The marijuana business was less risky than my parents' lifestyle, and carried less time if things went sideways. There wasn't as much danger as you see in the narcotics trade, and the profit margins were great from what I was already making. James lived a life that I saw as far more attainable, but still had the results I wanted.

# GROWING THROUGH IT

Modest by our standards from when I was growing up, James could choose between a Range Rover and a Bentley coupe he owned, and he stayed in a mansion in the hills of Encino. Or his more convenient luxury apartment on the Wilshire corridor in Westwood. It wasn't bad for just pushing a few pounds of leafy green bulbs every week. I planned on learning as much as I could from him and obtaining just as much—if not more.

"Yo! So we need someone to pick up the money," James informed me one evening at his plush pad as he cracked open a bottle of tequila and poured us some shots. Jason was unwilling to go, but I jumped at the opportunity, if not for the money but for the pure adrenaline rush. I could also prove myself and learn from the experience. Besides, I had come home from school to see my older brother Marlon, his friend Charles, and others count over a million dollars on many occasions.

I would make the most out of the trip, pick up the money, and return so we could do it again. It was easier than depositing the cash into different bank accounts in other people's names and having to go around and retrieve it, not to mention cheaper than having to pay each person a fee for the service or involve more folks than on a need-to-know basis about our activities. I even kept my mom in the dark about the very extent I went to handle this part of the business.

Returning home to Los Angeles from Detroit would prove difficult. After arriving, I met with my cousin "Tron," who was left in charge of coordinating with buyers of the shipments after his brother left to serve out his bid. Tron informed me there was over a hundred grand that needed to make its way back with me.

*How do we do that?* I thought. With the TSA and IRS policies on carrying large sums of cash and random searches, I couldn't just stuff it inside my suitcase and expect not to be stopped. This could spell trouble if they found the cash, and lead to it being confiscated.

"I got an idea!" Tron jumped up from his couch and ran out of the room before returning with duct tape.

"What the hell you gone do with that?" I asked, alarmed.

"Let's tape it to your body."

Puzzled, I just waited for any indication that it was a joke, but he stood before me, unflinching.

*"What?"* I responded, clearly bewildered.

"The metal detectors won't detect it, and they won't pat your stomach or anything."

It was the most outlandish proposal I'd ever considered, but it was possible. I didn't have much of a choice at this point. James was waiting back home for me to arrive, and I didn't want to back out of what I said I could handle, so I paused for a moment and agreed. "Let's do it!"

Stack after stack, Tron lined the bills across my stomach and then carefully applied the duct tape over them. Then he pulled me around as he wrapped the tape around my back. There wasn't enough room there. "Take off your pants," he ordered me.

*This is the craziest shit ever,* I thought as he wrapped more money on both legs.

"Okay, let's see."

I pulled on some oversized sweats and threw on a shirt. We both gazed over at the full-body mirror in the corner of the room, asking if it was obvious I was using myself as a cash mule.

"It may have just been easier paying for accounts," I said out loud.

"Too late for that," Tron responded.

I left and hopped into the car and headed back to my grand-mother Patricia's house, where my dad was also living and who planned on taking me to the airport.

# GROWING THROUGH IT

"Never let your right hand know what your left hand is up to," he used to tell me. Without wanting to worry him, or be scolded for my actions, I told him as little as possible. As for my grandmother, I told her I had come to visit her for the weekend and needed to return to school, but getting back to the West Coast would come with a few more hurdles.

As I arrived and walked over to check in at Detroit Metropolitan, the word CANCELED ran across the screens at the United desk for the flights to Los Angeles. *This has to be a joke,* I thought. *What the hell am I going to do with all this money strapped to my body?*

If I called my dad and asked him to pick me back up so I could wait to catch the next flight out the following morning, he might find out I was hiding a bundle of cash under my clothes, so I looked over at the screens before asking the attendant, "What's the closest you can get me to Los Angeles?"

"We have a flight to Las Vegas leaving at eight tonight," the attendant responded, appearing overwhelmed as she tried to attend to all the travelers now stuck because of what appeared to be unsafe weather conditions in California.

*Fuck it,* I thought. Just then, I made the snap decision to call my grandmother Carol, who was now staying at her vacation home for the fall in Las Vegas, to expect my arrival. No questions asked, she arrived to pick me up, once I landed in Vegas, where I would now have to sleep for the night, with money taped across my body. My grandmother spent most of her time out gambling, so she would hardly notice that I was stuck suffering as a cash mule until I could catch another flight to my final destination. Thankfully, she didn't notice a thing, and the next morning, she returned me to the airport.

I felt totally relieved to have made it past the TSA checkpoint and back to the city in time for James to buy more product to ship out the following week. Although I made it back safely, I took it as a sign that it would be the last time I'd attempt flying with money that way. Hopefully, for the next time, I'd be able to come up with another way to either bring the cash back or make a living entirely. Until then, this wouldn't stop us from devising more plans to make money.

I looked over my student portal at CSUN one evening to see that I had failed economics and would need to go see my counselor. While in his office, he informed me that two consecutive course failures meant I would need to attend a junior college and pick the grade up before I could continue my studies at the university. Shortly after that, I enrolled at Valley College with plans to pick up the grade.

When I felt sure I had lost interest in studying finance, I decided to enroll in a class in screenwriting, which I started with excitement. It would be easier to maintain a good grade and it was something I had been harboring a lifelong passion toward.

Upon driving into the student parking lot, a driver just ahead of me passed an open parking spot. I pulled in, quickly parked, and got out to head to class when the guy driving went in reverse and screamed, "Hey, you took my parking spot!"

"You passed it," I responded without giving it a second thought. Then I proceeded toward the school, where the unknown driver caught up to me quickly.

"Hey!" he called out to me again.

Turning around quickly, startled by his sudden reappearance behind me, I was thrown off by how swiftly he was able to find another parking spot and catch me in the pathway. "Bruh, don't run up behind me like that!" I yelled back at him as he towered above my five-foot-nine frame.

"That was my spot," he insisted.

I repeated he had passed the spot, and in doing so, I went ahead and took it, assuming he planned on exiting or had found another place to park. He couldn't possibly have reversed into the spot because the spaces for cars to drive by were too small and positioned at a diagonal to prevent people from backing into the spots, where the ticket person would be unable to see their parking permit. So I brushed the encounter off and headed to class, thinking, *Watch, with my luck, I probably have class with this clown.*

Sure enough, the irate driver was in my screenwriting class, and to make matters worse, the professor paired us off into groups of five, where we were grouped together.

After assessing the situation, I was quick to speak up. "Professor, I don't think this is going to work for me. This guy is harassing me about a parking spot," I said.

"Just try to work with him. I'm sure it'll be okay," the professor responded positively.

It didn't work out at all. Right in front of my face, this white boy began slandering me to the other group members over a parking spot that neither one of us owned—never mind the fact he was able to find another one moments later. They ignored him, and this must have gotten under his skin. He grabbed my book bag, which had my brand-new MacBook, which my mother had bought me before she left to do her time, along with a pair of Beats by Dre headphones stored inside it, and hurled it out of the room.

I followed him into the hallway and an uncontrollable rage came over me. I just knew he had broken my laptop and headphones, and I wanted him to pay, so I lunged toward him, getting a clean shot at the side of his face, before he took off calling me a "nigger," causing all the other students to spill out into the corridor to see what all the commotion was about.

Our professor ran over and I was pulled away when the sheriffs arrived; I gave them my side of the story.

"Well, he's pretty red," one of the officers concluded.

*Of course, he's red; he's white,* I told myself.

My one punch resulted in my being suspended from the school, forcing me to pull out of the course, thus ending my higher-education pursuits. The white guy taking my belongings and calling me a "nigger" didn't seem to matter. Because of this, I lost all interest in continuing with school and I completely dropped out. School was getting in the way of me making real money, anyway. I even went as far as believing God wanted me to succeed *without* a degree, to show that not only I, but others, could prevail without some stupid piece of paper saying I passed an economics or dumb screenwriting class. Besides, I had already been hindered from getting several industry jobs as it was.

*Who is going to pay my rent or cover all the other expenses we have?* I asked myself.

Now out of school, I wasn't able to see how this was going to affect me in the future. It was like I began to slowly drift into a life that was aimless. I started to go out more and spend less time thinking about a future that would bring stability. I wrote screenplays loosely based on our lives, sending them to my mom to critique, but she would simply respond that she didn't understand how to read the dialogue, and this would only push my dreams further away.

Doubt grew in me as things began to go awry, at first without notice. Losing my financial aid hurt my pockets, and it was a drastic hit to take. How was I going to pay my rent and survive? If the money from our secret business failed, it could mean disaster. What the hell was I going to do?

Rarely did I meet up with James to get the cut of profits that Jason and I were entitled to receive. As time went by, it became more and more frequent that Jason would show up and report that James was short, without a believable explanation.

"He said that you gave him the okay to borrow," Jason said to me one time.

After getting into a heated conversation with James, having believed the stories Jason told me, it came to light that his spending had spilled over into my funds, and delaying seeking the truth caused a rift between me and my one-time mentor and friend. Things seemed to be going great, and he was still doing quite well.

"How could we be coming up short?" I asked my brother before making the decision to pull the funds we pooled together. It was a fatal mistake that would cost us quite a lot more than I anticipated.

I'd visit my mom and, while in a heated game of Scrabble, relay the information that James seemed not to be trustworthy and I would handle things on my own. Not wanting us brothers to separate, or not have a connection, she insisted on his involvement, but things wouldn't turn out as hoped after Jason totaled his Range Rover one night from drunk driving and found himself behind bars.

"Just let it go! If they won't work to get it back, it's not your responsibility," my mom said, exhausted, on a call from prison. She was getting close to being able to come home and it became obvious that setbacks were becoming rampant. Jason and his girlfriend chucked over the responsibility of trying to get the truck out of impound and filing the insurance claim. After attempts to remedy the situation came to no avail, Mom insisted I leave it to them or let it go.

After losing their apartment for not paying the rent, they would soon be forced to move into my apartment. Things almost came to blows after I informed Jason that he would have to give the room up to Langston, who had already paid half the rent and supplied groceries. Jason didn't take the suggestion seriously and became visibly irritated. Fearing it would become a physical altercation, I backed down.

Jason was my brother, after all. What was I supposed to do? I couldn't put him out on the street. It was a conversation I failed to have with Langston, and it seemed to cause a rift in my once-prosperous friendship and partnership with him. Resentment began to harbor inside me when I would later find out Jason's girlfriend was also receiving payments from our shipment of marijuana and depositing them into her bank account.

The two lovebirds were splurging on Pizza Hut and Outback Steakhouse, while I struggled to pay rent, and I was now forced to share my car with them when they needed to make a run. It was enough to make me pack up and leave when the Department of Water and Power cut the lights off for nonpayment. I hoped it would get them to leave, and it did.

I shacked up in James's spare bedroom of his luxury apartment on Wilshire Corridor and dreamed of a day I would get things back in order and be able to live on my own again; but until then, I needed to figure out how to pay the electricity bill. I wasn't sure how to get out of this bind, so I pawned my mother's diamond ring, which took me over a year to get back out of a pawnshop. Embarrassed and ashamed, I kept it a secret and paid the rent, hoping to get back on my feet in a few short months.

However, things only seemed to go further into a downward spiral. Staying afloat solely from the money I had socked away, I'd eventually lose my car as well and had to pay the rent from the check received after the finance company sent the money left over from auctioning the car. It was the one saving grace that when my mom returned eventually, I was able to hold on to the apartment, assuring she had somewhere to go after being released. This was especially gratifying after receiving a notice in the mail that the town house she left to be managed by her so-called friend had fallen into foreclosure.

It was hard to figure out how I had managed to make it work for so long, but even harder for me to imagine being in a less fortunate circumstance. During my visits with Mom, I listened to her share how some women didn't know where their children were, or that the grandparents were too old to bring them to visit, and how many struggled or were stuck in the system. She told me many were taken away from their families for abuse and neglect by the Department of Children and Family Services. I was hardly neglected or abused, but I felt riddled with guilt from what appeared to be my own neglect. I had taken for granted what seemed to be a blessed situation that protected me for most of my life, and especially when I was confronted with taking on the responsibilities that she had trusted me with.

# Chapter 19

# Free at Last

*Corey's narration*
*2012*

**"I**'M FREE!" MY MOM EXCLAIMED AS SHE EMERGED FROM THE CAGE doors of the federal halfway home where she was assigned.

It felt like the perfect day to start a new year and the beginning of a new life. On January 1, 2012, there wasn't a cloud in the sky; and although it was the start of winter, the weather was decidedly pleasant. Wearing pink sweats, she gave me a huge hug before receiving a warm embrace from Lisa, who had brought her flowers. They began to weep in joy as the cameras rolled from inside the Porsche Panamera, which was loaned to Lisa B for the first shoot of the promptly titled *BMF Wives* sizzle reel. Due to federal restrictions against recording on government property, the cameraman, "Paper," as he's known, recorded from the back, making sure not to be seen as we filmed.

I was now officially a college dropout and struggling to make ends meet. Still, the hope for the future was strong enough for both me and my mom. During her time in prison, I took some screenwriting classes after writing a script loosely based on our lives about a high-profile record executive and his family moving to Los Angeles and how their world becomes thrown upside down. I would later discover my mom had similar ambitions about telling her story.

While she took on a low-paying concierge job at the Topanga Mall in Woodland Hills, California, I enrolled at the Los Angeles Film School and learned the basics of filmmaking. While I believed in the power of her story, an old family associate of Terry's suggested that we look for other women to join us. In came Lisa, who became a main supporter to our cause, and the second lead in the docuseries, which we planned to pitch around Hollywood.

Using Lisa's connections in the industry, we were able to snag David Weintraub as a producer. David was Ray J's manager, and he'd previously experienced some success in the television world. His claim to fame was: "Aaron gave me a million dollars when I was just twenty years old." Of course, everyone knows Aaron Spelling was a legend in television for producing shows such as *The Love Boat, Dynasty,* and *Charlie's Angels.* It surely felt as if we were making headway—and fast. All the days of writing and watching HBO's *Entourage* seemed about to pay off. Not to mention the struggle of surviving and losing everything, being vindicated, would spearhead us into giving hope to others with big dreams being led down the wrong path.

"No studio is going to give you guys a budget for this," producer after producer said. After several attempts and cast swaps, the promise of a deal seemed to evaporate. "We have decided not to extend the holding agreement," David's business partner informed Lisa and my mom during a meeting at Gower Studios one morning.

That was it. The dream was dead. David had also lost interest, so it seemed my mom and I would be relegated to a mall job and a useless college degree from a technical school. Doubt hung heavily in the air around us.

"What are we going to eat?" I asked my mom.

She sat on the sofa, appearing to be in profound thought. *Perhaps in a deep well of self-pity?* I thought.

"I don't have any money." Her words penetrated like sharp arrows and landed at my feet with a thud as my heart sank. I had never heard her utter the words that she didn't have any money, and a cloud of sadness came over me.

*How can I change this?*

I had never been in such a predicament, and neither had she. I'm sure my mom couldn't remember the last time, if any, that she'd ever come to the conclusion she was flat broke, but the day had finally arrived. It was a gut punch to my confidence and faith. I moved across the living room to share an embrace of reassurance that we would figure it out. I had no clue how; and evidently, she didn't, either.

The woman sitting before me was certainly not the woman I knew when I was growing up. She was wholly someone else. Her confidence gone, the woman with all the answers was now fresh out of money and down on her luck. She didn't have the answers anymore, let alone any idea of what to even eat.

*How did we get here?* I thought.

I not only let my mom down, but myself as well. I honestly believed I would be in a better position by the time she came home—or at least I would have a bachelor's degree from Northridge. However, that had dissolved as quickly as I had started. I only lasted two semesters at CSUN before being ousted to pick up my grades at a junior college.

"We have chosen not to extend our holding agreement," David's partner had broken the news during the last failed pitch meeting.

The networks just didn't get it, or the story was skewing too urban for some of their audiences. After expressing their deep interest in the project, other networks would use that explanation, conveying how the subject was compelling, but they were hesitant to take the risk.

David's team would lose faith and interest in trying to make the show work. We would be left to lick the wounds of what felt like defeat and a major setback. What would we do now? I was making little profit from my small marijuana business, and things were already tight and becoming tighter. It felt like the carpet had been pulled from right under my feet.

I had been a rich kid and was now living as a poor adult, with no hopes for the future. So much for all the things my mom taught me before turning herself in at the prison. The only thing I was able to hold on to was my apartment, where my brother Jason, my mom, and I all lived.

"Let's just do it ourselves!" Lisa said passionately one day. While out to lunch, she and my mother discussed where to go from here. After David's production company decided not to renew their contract, they were left with the decision to either give up or keep going.

*Let's keep going!*

They made up their minds and enlisted Paper to film the process and began searching for other women to join them. Soon Temeka, one of Wayne's longtime love interests, and Johnell "Big Meech's wifey" were cast to be a part of this uphill battle of recognition. Johnell, a dancer out of Atlanta, seemingly met Meech from the letters she wrote him while he was serving time in prison. Lisa thought it would be great to add her, to begin mending fences between the two factions and possibly bring some light-hearted drama to the sizzle reel—and eventually a show, if it was picked up.

None of us had any experience producing a show, but with my genuine passion for storytelling and my own ambitions of working in the film industry, I was enlisted to help bridge the storyline and edit the footage Paper so skillfully filmed. Armed with the standard-issue MacBook Pro and editing software from my enrollment at the LAFS, we took the tools available to us and began to piece together a compelling sizzle reel.

"No studio is going to put up a budget for this." Executives and producers all over town doubted the concept of not only the show, but dramatizing the story of BMF at all. To me, they seemed skeptical or even scared of pitching a show about some Black drug dealers who made a lot of money and then went to prison.

That didn't deter me, and neither did failing to pay the Los Angeles Film School for the last year of my education. Just $3,600 shy of the full $21,000 tuition, I had run out of options when I was turned down for a loan, and grants wouldn't cover the rest. Feeling desperate, I went to my father, who was back home in Detroit. "No, you'll never work in film" is the only thing that stuck in my head when he declined to help me cover the rest or co-sign a loan to prevent me from being forced to pull out of the school until I could pay for it.

"It must be paid in full before you can continue," my counselor relayed while we sat in her office, desperately trying to remedy the situation or come up with a solution. I hoped I could pay in installments, but no. They wanted every last dime before they would allow me to move forward with classes.

"We don't offer any screenwriting courses here. Why are you here?" a professor asked me during a session on camera work.

*Why am I here?* I thought. Fed up, I decided to pull out and prove my father wrong, and also show the school administration that I could do it without them.

I affirmed to myself that I would excel at my dream without a formal education. With the little I learned about editing and my new MacBook, I would prove it to everyone.

The weight of putting a sizzle reel together was hard to carry with Lisa B, the other woman, and my mom breathing down my neck. They had decided to just drop the reel on YouTube and see what the results were. The anticipation was unbearable. What if I failed? What if no one liked it or, worse, no one watched it? What if the more experienced industry folks were correct with what they said to us? I didn't want to think about how not only would I be perceived as a failure, but my mom would be, too. We would fail in front of everyone.

It was during the process of filming the sizzle reel that I wanted to focus on our evolution and redemption. After being released from federal custody, it was difficult for my mom to find work, and as a felon, she took the first job she was offered. The Topanga Mall welcomed her as a concierge and liaison for all the shoppers who entered the mall; but beyond that, it also brought the opportunity to give back and birthed the idea for her own foundation.

Christmas was just around the corner and Westfield's Topanga Mall was hosting a fundraiser and toy drive for less fortunate children. I proposed the idea to my mom that we join this opportunity to give back, but also film that side of her, to show the true motivation for wanting to tell her story on a platform.

I then suggested the concept to Lisa. "So I got something for us. There's this walk-with-Santa event going on at the mall and I think we should do it."

Lisa didn't react as positively to the proposal as we did, but she begrudgingly agreed.

"Okay, it's for the kids!" Lisa responded, sounding enthused.

"Yeah, for the kids," my mom said endearingly.

It was done. We wrapped on the shoot; and after painstakingly working on the final edit, color correction, and music score, I uploaded the reel to YouTube and pressed broadcast. It went live and instantly blew up on the Internet. Every major urban blog had it posted, and my mother's phone began to ring within minutes. It gathered over seven hundred thousand views within a few weeks and production companies started calling.

Eventually talk show host Ricki Lake had her producers call us. They wanted to feature a segment about women dating men in prison, featuring Lisa, Johnell, and my mother on her show.

Still running with the excitement from participating in the Santa event, I began to think of how we could shed light on the countless children affected by incarceration and inspire others in similar, or less fortunate, situations as me. After my father was incarcerated, my family took part in helping to raise me. I was only two years old when he went away. As I grew up, my grandmother Patricia took me to the Museum of African American History, Detroit Institute of Art, and went on field trips with me; my aunt Edith would bring me with her own daughters to see Disney on Ice and monster truck rallies; my mom worked as a single mother to provide a stable home. I wanted to do the same for my own niece Malana while her father, Marlon, was away.

The idea of doing a visual PSA felt like a great way to convey the message we both experienced, even though I never knew my niece's true thoughts about how it affected her not having her father around as she grew up. I knew from my own experience that it's hard seeing other children's fathers come for parent-teacher conferences and other events, and your own is absent—and you're ashamed to share where they truly are. Now that my mom was gearing up to tell her testimony, I wanted us to be a part of the journey, in our own way, by producing a video with my niece portraying a young girl who was a silent victim of a widespread issue.

# Chapter 20
# Sylent Heart

*2013 and beyond*

URING MY STINT IN PRISON, I'D SEEN A LOT OF MOTHERS THERE unable to contact or provide for their children. Corey's father had also been in jail. So I wanted to help kids like my son have the opportunities and resources to pursue some of the things they were interested in doing. Corey and his niece were going to produce a video about children and incarcerated parents. We spoke about it, and we were on the same wavelength. That's how he and I started our nonprofit Sylent Heart Foundation. From at-risk children, we'd subsequently expand to caring for the homeless and at-risk women.

I wasn't without my own doubts in the beginning. Money was tight and I wasn't sure how we could help, or even find, children in similar circumstances. "We don't have any money. We can't just do it!" I said to Corey in frustration.

Corey wouldn't take my words as defeat. He insisted, "We don't need money to start!" Adamant that a nonprofit just needed to be set up and could raise the money it needed, he made the first initial call to a Chuck E. Cheese in Dearborn, Michigan, where they agreed to contribute 15 percent of all sales made during our fundraiser.

*There it was!* We had our first sponsor, and all we had to do was get people to show up and, without their donating a dollar to us directly, the children's restaurant would cut a check to Sylent Heart to provide resources for children in need.

As soon as my friend Kari learned about our mission, she jumped in to help me. Utilizing her connections from being an LA native, we hit the pavement and drove downtown, where it was decided to go further than just a fundraiser. We would actually make a difference to children that fall who were returning to school. Wholesalers downtown would cut us a break and donate five hundred backpacks, and we received over $25,000 in cash donations, which went to filling the bags with all the supplies needed to give the kids a head start to their new school year. We stuffed pens, pencils, rulers, notebooks, loose-leaf paper, calculators, and dictionaries into the backpacks.

It was truly amazing and was way beyond what we had first envisioned. Thinking of the women I spent time with behind bars who wondered where their children were, we started a campaign for people to write and email us the most deserving family that needed help. From that outreach, we stumbled upon a remarkable young girl out of Detroit who was raising three young boys alone, since her husband was serving a thirty-year sentence. She was unable to provide basic necessities or afford a phone for him to call his young boys in order to keep in touch, so we were able to purchase and donate a phone with several months paid up front. It wouldn't change the world, but it was a start. Those little boys, just like my son, were living with pain and hurt in silence.

That's where the inspiration originally came from for the name of our foundation. Sylent Heart was about the silent victims we were now serving and the communities that don't have a voice, the decisions that have rippling effects on them and their loved ones. Despite not knowing anyone, and having no practical idea how to start a foundation, we came together and were able to help a good number of mothers and their children prepare for school, lightening the load as the necessities for new clothes and food weighed down on families. I felt a strong sense of accomplishment from my journey coming full circle. After many nights of listening to the women I was in prison with, I got to know and love them all. The experience really opened my eyes to how the system and my own deeds helped break down family dynamics. It was now the time for me to help repair the damage and bridge a gap for those women and children who shared similar stories.

Thinking back on it, when I had been made camp leader, it hadn't been a punishment at all. It had been another lesson to prepare me to help a lot more people on the outside.

That same year, in 2013, my stepfather, Emerson, became ill and was admitted to the hospital after he had difficulty breathing. After having X-rays, it was discovered that he was in the last stages of lung cancer. Doctors gave him only a few months to prepare for the inevitable. He was placed into hospice, where he prepared to say his last goodbyes.

Corey, my mother, and I would drive to Ann Arbor to visit him as he lay hardly conscious, connected to numerous pieces of monitoring equipment and a breathing machine, which helped oxygen travel into his lungs. My mother, Carol, moved over to Emerson's side and rubbed his head. She showed little emotion and stood stoic as she watched her love—a man she had adored for decades—begin to fade away.

As I stood at the edge of the bed, peering over him, he opened his eyes and gazed up into mine, like he had never seen me before. Silently he held up his hand and I moved over to the side of the bed where he could grasp my hand. Never looking away from me, he uttered, "You are so beautiful . . ."

Tears began streaming down my face as my mother moved closer, wanting him to notice her in the corner. Fishing for her own compliment, she asked, "What about me?"

He closed his eyes and fell back into a peaceful slumber; my compliment is the last thing I recall him saying. Although at the time, I found my mom wanting her own validation to be hilarious, it did strike a chord with me after all those years of his never actually commenting on or acknowledging my beauty. As he lay on his deathbed, and just before departing this world, he awoke to impart those last thoughtful words, which I had wanted to hear from him so badly when I was a child. It had taken almost forty years to hear the words that I so desperately needed to hear—that he actually loved and valued me, even though for so many years his actions said otherwise.

When it really counted, his departing words proved how much he loved and appreciated me, even though he teased me a lot when I was growing up. Losing my father while I was in the prison life was a hole that I could never fill. Being able to have closure and feel like I had made Emerson proud before he left us reinforced my resilience and confidence that I would make it through this tough time.

Things would slowly take a turn in a new direction, with the support of my family, especially from my mother and son Corey. I began to see a new life working with at-risk women and children, and we started to garner attention from the *BMF Wives* sizzle reel. In time, I was able to secure a higher-paying job at Medtronic, a company that built medical devices for patients, and was fielding offers from new production companies. That's not to say it didn't come without its own resistance and backlash, though.

With my past record, I found that getting a job at Medtronic wasn't easy; and shortly after several failed attempts to secure a better income, I changed my name back to my ex-husband's, making it easier not to disclose my conviction. I leaned back into my past ways of leading a double life and creating my own narrative to my co-workers. It wasn't ideal, but with money tight and my prospects low, it seemed to be the only solution at the time.

How did they expect anyone to survive, let alone live a positive and productive life, after leaving custody if no one was willing to give us a second chance? It seemed an unfair quirk in the system— one that was designed to set us up for failure—and for many women like me, they did fail.

As more and more attention came from the sizzle reel all over the Internet, I began to fear the company I worked for, and lied to, would begin to take notice, or that one of my co-workers would discover my secret. It felt like I was waiting for the roof to cave in, just as it had when I lay in my bed in Mulholland at night waiting for the Feds to come knocking. Could I still be falling into the hole that once having been in prison meant always remaining in prison? I mean, could things get any worse? I sometimes caught myself allowing doubt to creep into my mind.

Producers expressed interest in our reel, but they still had their doubts; and the fighting among the ladies began to overshadow our shared goal. None of us were willing to part with the idea of being co-creators or executive producers, and the industry was against allowing us a say or input on how they would portray us or steer my new life. It seemed unimaginable after all the time I spent helping others, building up these so-called loves of my life, and then being sent to prison to serve time for things I didn't have any control over. That sounded like the oft-repeated definition of insanity: doing the same things repeatedly, but expecting a different result.

A woman by the name of Tammy Cowins, and I had never met her, also felt she had the right to control and weigh in on what I could do. Claiming to own the rights to BMF, and being Demetrius's business partner, she took interviews and dispelled rumors about our possible show. She made calls to get it shut down.

"How dare this bitch!" I said aloud to Corey. I read an online blog article where she claimed I had no involvement with Meech or his brother, and I couldn't do a show without her say.

"She didn't do a day in prison!" I shouted.

Tammy seemed to have come from nowhere. She possibly could have been one of the countless pen pals Meech met while incarcerated or maybe a club troll he met during his many nights clubbing in Atlanta. She had no prior run-ins with the law; and from what I could gather, no real experience running the streets or calling shots when it came to the politics that governed the drug trade. She was just some Jezebel who got lucky and hit her mark and was now using Meech for clout and acclaim.

"Where were all these people when they were giving out time?" I wanted to know. They were nowhere to be found, but suddenly people from all over were the Black Mafia Family. Tammy included was now clamoring to get a piece of the pie, without ever putting in the work or sacrifice. Ultimately she managed to get ahold of me via cell phone and attempted to intimidate me with threats.

"Bitch, fuck you, and your kids will see when they take you back to jail!" she screamed through the phone. Not taking it as a serious threat, I hung up the phone and shrugged her off. The truth would come out eventually and she couldn't stop anything, but she sure did try. Keeping to her promise, I received a call from my probation officer the next day informing me that I needed to come in. *Fuck! This bitch actually filed a report on me,* I thought. It was quite crafty and took a lot of work to go and find out who my actual probation officer was that I needed to report to. It appeared as though this wasn't her first time, judging by the amount of time it took for my probation officer to receive the complaint.

"They're going to need to send more proof," Mrs. Prado said flatly. Relief rushed over my body, washing away all the fear that had taken over as I arrived at the federal probation office to answer the report that Tammy had threatened me with.

Luckily, Mrs. Prado saw right through Tammy's blatant lie and attempt to manipulate the system and set me up. "You're almost done. You've been doin' good. Just try your best to stay clear of these people," my probation officer warned, reassuring me she had my back against fraudulent reports and those just looking to set me back again. Clearly, there were people not happy with the fact I was making a change in my life for the better. They were not pleased that I was determined to turn what was once a negative into a mechanism for positive change in the world.

I wouldn't wish prison on my worst enemy, and I was sure Tammy wasn't one to spar with, especially during this time and in such a precarious situation when it came to my freedom. Corey eventually took the sizzle reel down from YouTube and only showed it to interested parties, expressing the need to focus on just me and my mission. He maintained that I had a strong enough story, and an ensemble cast took away from the allure of my own narrative and mission.

Corey and I haven't always agreed, which is par for the course for those who return after being away for an extended period of time. I had to learn to adjust to this new person he was growing into, while he had to get reacquainted with the woman he thought he knew before I left for prison. This reunion between us was easier said than done. Every family must deal with the consequences that come with welcoming back returning family members.

Corey had become accustomed to coming and going as he pleased and making his own decisions. Now here I was, trying to be the mother I was before I left, wanting to know where he was headed, what people he would be with, and when I should expect his return. How outlandish it was that all of a sudden I thought he needed to report his every move to me, after I had been away for so long.

As far as Corey was concerned, in his eyes, it was totally unnecessary. How much had this young man changed since I last lived with him? Sure, he was quite capable of doing many things on his own, but he still relied on me to call and give advice when I could. Bu then we started having issues seeing eye to eye about the most basic decisions.

"We can't afford that!" he'd yell at me as I ordered a pricey meal at a restaurant.

"Listen, I want to eat what I want to eat," I'd shoot back.

When it came to certain things, I was unflinching about the price or ramifications, coming up with simple justifications of how it made me feel or might not impact us in the long term. What would eating out or buying a new handbag do to push us forward or hinder us? Corey always seemed to be planning ahead, while I thought I could always figure it out.

"Don't post that!" Corey nagged at me, seeming to want to control what I posted on Instagram. He regularly chided me about inappropriate or offensive pictures that I figured were harmless. It wouldn't dawn on me until I received a call from Mayor Eric Garcetti's office that people were watching.

"Hello, Mrs. Welch. We have been watching you on Instagram and like the message you are sending. We want you to be a part of a program we are working on."

The Los Angeles mayor actually had his people reach out to bring me on board to be a part of a coalition to get the box removed on job applications that wanted applicants to check if they had ever been convicted of a crime or were on probation. Prison reform seemed to slowly be picking up traction and the mayor's office and others in politics were beginning to shed light on the discriminatory practices that go with asking if you have any prior convictions. Speaking from my own experience, I discovered it was nearly impossible to get a decent job, or even an interview, before I started using my married name, which wasn't connected with my time served.

The connotations of being an ex-felon make employers avoid

those applicants and avoid people who just want to provide for their family and for themselves. Unfortunately, this causes many to fall back into a life of crime and become repeat offenders. I did not realize it until then, but my son was right. I needed to adjust my page and post more of the positive things we were doing and the messages I wanted to share with other women like me. It didn't take knowing anyone or having an abundance of money to exact change. It was the drive that I had that helped me bring change in my life and into the lives of countless others.

A bill was successfully passed outlawing the right to ask potential employees about their criminal past, and we would go on to hold several job fairs that resulted in hiring one thousand people through reentry programs with participating companies. Fortune 500 companies slowly began to see that untapped talent lies in unlikely places; and in order to get people who think outside the box, sometimes you have to look inside the boxes of prison walls.

As we worked together, I discovered and learned more things about my son that were difficult for us both to navigate in the beginning. Corey, who was born two weeks late, arriving on the day of my birthday, came into this world to become my best friend and biggest supporter. He was also my greatest challenge. We had a great relationship before I turned myself in, and it seemed to be threatened when I returned home. He seemed to be a man who was totally different than I remembered. Sure, he was still my baby, who came almost every weekend to visit me, and to make sure there was money on my books, and the bills I left behind were paid, but he had noticeably changed.

"I'm gay!" Corey blurted out nervously in a drunken, slurred voice. It was during a night out with some of his college friends at a bar named Buffalos, in Santa Monica, that he made that startling reveal.

In all honesty, it came from left field. It was the last thing I expected, nor was it welcoming news to hear. I didn't take it as well as I could have, but from my experience in prison, and growing up in the inner city, it did not bring comfort to know what he would go through and how others most likely would treat him, knowing his lifestyle. It seemed to weigh down on him heavily, and I attributed a lot of his decision-making from having been encumbered by what he thought others might think, especially because of who his parents were and what the family represented.

There is some shame in how I handled it in the moment. It took time for us both to communicate in a healthy manner in a way he felt comfortable expressing some of the things he was going through. There were times when I found it difficult to sometimes see his viewpoint.

Still, I think how much this secret must have psychologically damaged him, especially while I was gone. All the numerous times he came to visit me and shared some of his exploits in the club and the difficulties he'd had with friends and the opposite sex must have made it all the much harder to talk about, but easier to compartmentalize because I wasn't around to see. Now that I was back, it proved to be a hindrance to who he was and how he lived. I clearly had a great deal to catch up on and work through with both my boys, and it wouldn't be easy. Adjusting to a new life was hardly a walk in the park, and I know that their growing up accustomed to a certain lifestyle, and then losing it, was a hard thing for both of them. It came with its own ridicule from those they believed were their friends and supported them.

"What happened between you two has nothing to do with us." Corey expressed repeatedly that my discomfort about his friendship with Jessica's son, and him visiting the apartment often, was something that caused soreness for me, but it wasn't Corey's problem. Here I was, switching off sleeping in the bed or on the couch with my youngest son, while Corey's closest friend's mother was a culprit in embezzling money out of my mortgage, causing me to lose my home before I could return.

Every time I looked at him, it served as a reminder of the huge mistake I had made in trusting someone over my son, and it was now happening in reverse. Corey was now choosing his loyalty to his friend, who was there for him while I was gone, despite his mother not being the friend I expected her to be. It felt like a betrayal and an affront to me. How could he even come over here and not feel a way about our situation as he made himself a bowl of the cereal I just bought?

"He has a mother and a job. Could you at least ask him to replace the cereal?" I asked Corey.

Corey dug in his heels. I could tell it seemed like a petty request to make, and it was so contrary to his upbringing, and almost hypocritical of me to ask someone to replace the food they ate. I always tried to instill in my boys that if we had food, anyone could eat it; and here I was now, counting Cheerios. Corey's insistence that things between them had nothing to do with us would be unwavering, until my run-in with Jessica at a premiere party for the show *Empire*.

The encounter would spark a bold piece of gossip spread by Jessica that I had arrived at the star-studded event with several women, and we were prepared to have her jumped. It was another incredible lie by a perpetrator who stole my home right from underneath me, but Corey's friendship would be an unlikely casualty in the ensuing debacle. It would come about from a girl in the neighborhood, where they had grown up, who informed him that not only was Jessica spreading this nasty lie, but her son was also attempting to slander my name.

Blindsided by the news, Corey seemed to be deeply affected with anger and confusion by what he was told, and the question of loyalty was tossed to the forefront. Had he been disloyal to me or purely betrayed by a once-close ally? As it turned out, Corey wasn't the only one who suffered from these major lies. My middle son, Jason, had moved on to another relationship, but he slowly crept further into a life of alcohol, drug abuse, and depression. He became isolated, only dealing with his wife and kids; and although he was a great father, Jason had a deep hole inside him, which no one seemed able to reach or repair.

Now, Corey always found a way to turn a negative into a positive, no matter the circumstances, and this situation turned out no different. Out of a fateful run-in while out shopping for shoes with Ben, Leah Butler's brother-in-law, who was a close friend of Jessica and her son's, Corey confronted him in the middle of the Topanga Mall about the gossip and the lies being spread about me.

"How dare you? You should be trying to build people up, not break them down, especially having been to prison yourself!" Corey screamed. He went on to accuse the man of being a snitch and to say other choice words.

"Corey, you're right, I did. Nor am I ashamed, but I do hear what you are saying, and I agree," Ben responded in a reasonably calm manner.

It would be a short while later that Ben would call Corey and ask to be connected with me. This time, it wouldn't be to discuss more gossip or throw more verbal jabs, but to invite me to be a part of an initiative to give back to the homeless.

"We're doing a pop-up feeding the homeless event with the BIG3," Ben informed me.

The BIG3, co-founded by Ice Cube in 2017, was a league that was garnering attention for putting retired NBA stars back on the court. This charity event felt like another huge opportunity to help those in need and to repair some of the damage that had been caused by the years of destruction from the drugs we had peddled to the very population that was most in need of resources. It included thirteen cities, and I personally helped organize several of the events in Los Angeles, Miami, Detroit, and St. Louis.

We didn't just feed the people; we provided haircuts, clothes, fun games, prizes, and free employment resources to those in dire need. This led to recognition, with Ice Cube receiving a key to the city in Miami-Dade County from the mayor, but it would be in my hometown where I received the highest praise and sense of accomplishment.

## 2018

July 13, 2018, wasn't just any other day for me. On this day, I felt a great sense of accomplishment rushing through my body and I was beyond ecstatic as I stood looking out from a traveling stage onto a gazing crowd. City Councilwoman Mary Sheffield's voice echoed as she spoke into the microphone and thanked me for my contributions to the city. The sun beamed down on me as I was awarded the Spirit of Detroit plaque. Surrounded by friends, family, and supporters, I had just pulled off my most notable charitable event to date.

We pulled off the homeless pop-up event, a nationwide tour, in partnership with Ice Cube's BIG3 NBA legends league, without a hitch. We fed more than one thousand individuals, provided haircuts, passed out hygiene kits and clothes, and provided games, music, and entertainment to the inner city. Standing on a temporary stage, as I looked out onto the crowd and the vacant lot, which we had transformed into an epicenter full of tents providing food, a dance floor, info booths for dental and health programs, and a makeshift barbershop, a surreal feeling vibrated throughout my entire body.

I mean, to have gone from breaking the law to this! Somehow I had managed to do a full 180-degree turn. Doing charitable work and working with policymakers and corporations to make a difference for the next generation looked good on me.

In retrospect, it's almost unbelievable where I've ended up. I have spent many days wondering, *What is it about me that made people treat me this or that way? What was it about me that I'd end up in certain circumstances?*

It's a drastic change from where my life started. I'm no longer standing in the shadow of a powerful man or masquerading as some stay-at-home mom of a successful executive. It's a far cry from my days of running the streets, hitting store after store with bad checks or returning stolen items for cash. My path has been made clear. My purpose and power seem all but obvious, and where I am headed all but inevitable.

# Chapter 21
# Staying in the Middle

*2016 and beyond*

IN 2016, I BECAME REALLY ILL AFTER A FUN BOOZE-FILLED WEEKEND IN Las Vegas, where I had tried my best to keep up with Corey and his friends while tagging along with producer Jermaine Dupri, who invited us out to experience him tearing the club up spinning at the Encore resort hotel. After returning to Los Angeles, Corey rushed me to the hospital, where the doctors, at first, were clueless as to what was the cause of the excruciating pain in my abdomen. Hospitalized for over a month, I was eventually diagnosed with acute pancreatitis.

This sickness is frequently not caught in time. Its causes are complex and varied, leaving many medical professionals baffled as to when and how it flares up. My doctor rejoiced that I came when I had; if I had waited any longer, the small but vital organ could have exploded and caused me to die. I again found myself reliant on the support of Corey and my mother. *This isn't how things should be.*

A young man should be able to live his life and figure things out, and, instead, Corey was here by my side, every step of the way.

My mother, still the stalwart, supported me through this time, even though she was trying to adjust to the loss of my stepfather. Since coming home from prison, I'd seen how much this woman, who'd never seemed invested in me as a kid, truly loved and cared about me. We traveled and did everything together, often talking two or three times a day. While things were really hard following my release, getting sick was even worse. Mom was my backbone, always saying, "Watch, it's going to get better."

It was still hard to believe, after all we had been through recently, that things were going to get better. Besides, Marlon was still in prison and fighting a separate case that was not being run concurrent with the BMF indictment. It appeared that he would have to serve additional time—unless a miracle happened—and a judge would hear his case and exonerate him from the additional time. The guilt weighed heavily on me even more while I lay sick in a hospital bed.

*How would my sons survive without me? What will become of Marlon and my granddaughter, once he was released?*

Without me being around, there was no one there to support them. It reminded me of the countless other women and men out there who were without voices. Who would speak up for them? How could we fight the unfair justice system and the racial biases that undoubtedly come along with it?

I would have to get better and do more to fight. There was no other option but to follow everything my doctor recommended and stick to it. No more alcohol; no heavy oils like butter, cheese, olive oil; no delectable salmon or other fish like that. They are all too harsh for my pancreas to break down, so I would have to follow a strict diet and monitor what I ate and how I lived my life from now on. It would be a far cry from how I behaved before and a clear sign from God that yet again I had been spared. There was more for me to do—not only for my children, but for the millions of other minorities in and out of those prison walls.

# STAYING IN THE MIDDLE

Marlon's case would push me to learn more about the law and different motions that could help to benefit him and others in similar situations. Taking what I had learned in all my free time in prison reading lawbooks, I began to network and pick other brains for knowledge. I pursued further research into how to help our own situations, which led me to file a grievance against his attorney, who totally failed him in his trial proceedings. Chills went through my body as I realized how many other men were probably represented by criminal attorneys who sought only a quick payday from their guilty clients. These lawyers walked away without any thought to the time they so willfully allowed their clients to serve, while they got to go home and be a part of their own children's and families' lives.

Returning to work one afternoon at the mall, I crossed through Nordstrom, where I would run into an old friend Cynthia. Cynthia was a kind girl and she called out my name, breaking me away from my deep thoughts.

"Toni, hey!"

I held steady, pretending to be happy and excited to be working at the mall, but thoughts about how to survive and where to go from my low-paying job as mall concierge tormented me day and night.

"Hey, girl!" I answered back.

Dressed in my uniform, I felt embarrassed and ashamed that the woman she once saw living the high life in the hills, driving expensive cars and wearing designer clothes, had now been reduced to waiting on all the other women who could shop and spend money on all the things I used to be able to afford.

"How are you?"

It felt like a loaded question. How had I been? *Struggling*, I thought, and my lips formed the answer, but I fought the temptation. My emotions began to get the best of me; before I knew it, I burst into tears and began sobbing.

"Oh, my God! Honey, what's wrong?" Cynthia asked.

*What isn't wrong?* I thought. I just came home from prison, was sleeping on my son's couch, struggled to pay the rent, and was working at the mall. This was a place I once loved to go and shop in, until I couldn't. Now it felt like an exile or the very bottom of the hole I tried so hard to avoid. I couldn't hold it in anymore. As she embraced me, I felt relieved to show such a vulnerable side of me, even if it was the last thing I had wanted to do.

"Whatever it is, it will get better. God got you," she said reassuringly.

Cynthia was right! I had made it through prison and had overcome everything that was put before me. This would be no different, no matter how difficult it seemed. It was a chance encounter with an old friend that brought me comfort when I most needed it, but had least wanted to admit it. In that instance, I realized how bottled up I kept things and some of the personal trials I was going through. I realized that I couldn't lie or pretend everything was okay when it wasn't. And for damn sure, I came to the grim realization that I couldn't change anything if I didn't acknowledge it and have faith in God and in myself.

After moving into a new apartment and piecing together the furniture while Corey was away in his room working on the *BMF Wives* sizzle reel, Kari and I poured ourselves a drink, a light glass of white wine to celebrate another accomplishment. Per the doctor's orders I could have just a pinch of wine here and there and now was just the time.

We settled into the sofa before she gazed over at me and asked, "Damn, girl, how do you get through it?"

"By staying in the middle," I responded.

She squinted her eyes and leaned in, waiting for a better explanation of what the middle was, and where it could possibly be.

"Sometimes I see it as me driving down the highway between the mountains and the ocean. As long as I keep straight ahead, I can't fall down the hill or swerve in the water and drown," I explained to her.

Her eyes became big as I finished by saying, "Sometimes I see my life as this journey, sorta like this dream that would torment me at night. I used to just drive blindly and not see the danger ahead, but now I stay focused on my goals."

It sounded like a good metaphor, even if I had just thought of it on a whim. It brought clarity to my own questions about that nightmare that had kept me up for so many nights, years before. That dream had me spending days thumbing through religion books and other ones about dreams, trying to find an interpretation of what it symbolized. Although it seems so simple now, to me, it was some mystifying message that had left me confounded for years: A message meant to help her had the double effect of helping me see what I had been looking past for too long.

My phone rang repeatedly, lighting up my screen with the same 310 area code, and a man by the name of Datari Turner left several voice messages.

"Hi, Ms. Welch, I received a link to a video about you and your association to BMF and was interested in setting up a meeting."

Datari was one of the creative executives over at Entertainment One. After all the failed attempts and false starts, I was hesitant to call back or have a sit-down with him.

"Toni, this is just the beginning," Kari had said that night in my living room. Her words complemented my mother's reassurance that things would work out if I just sat back and had patience. *Just stayed in the middle.* God would work things out, so I called back with reluctance, willing to at least hear what they had to say.

"We want to produce a show around you and give you executive producer credit on it. I know how much you've been through and how much this means to you and us as well," Tara Long said persuasively.

Tara was the head of development at Entertainment One. Although she wasn't Black, nor had she done any time in prison, she understood the hardships women go through and believed in my story, along with Datari. I agreed to develop a new show based off what we had done with *BMF Wives,* and without the drama of the other women or the past life I was desperate to put behind me.

Things began to look up and I was now signed to one of the largest producers of reality shows in the industry. This was the company that had created the likes of the Housewives series, *Growing Up Hip Hop,* and *Braxton Family Values.* I was in a class of high achievers and making my own way for once—and it wasn't a man who helped me do that. Nor was I helping someone else find their inner strength. I was finally doing it *for myself,* and finding a voice for the other women I was seeking to help.

# Chapter 22
# The Weight of Responsibility

*Corey's narration*
*2005 and beyond*

"**M**Y FATHER IS IN PRISON," TRENT BLURTED OUT AS WE SAT smoking in his grandparents' garage one early morning. Trent was my friend since high school. Having met through my brother Jason, he showed me the ropes when I went into ninth grade, as he was a year older and the person who introduced me to a lot of things and people.

Trent had never confided in me the fact his father was also doing time until I had co-founded Sylent Heart with my mother. It seemed such a simple thing to discuss, but once he revealed the truth, I realized how hard it is to talk about such a thing, even for me. I spent my entire life concealing the truth from my class-mates and anyone on the outside so that it became second na-ture. Until that day, I was blinded to how difficult it was holding that in—not only for him, but for myself, too.

"Wow, you just now telling me. I kind of figured," I added.

I hadn't *really* figured that out, but once he told me, it seemed quite obvious all these years his father had to be away. He had

185

come up with lavish stories about traveling and his father working in the industry. It was suspect that in more than ten years, I had never met his father or heard Trent ever say he spent the holidays with him, or was going away on vacation with him or his mother. Trent lived with his grandparents, which should have been a dead giveaway, but I guess I was too busy carrying the weight of my own family secrets to notice.

Trent kept up a good façade, although it was obvious he didn't have much money. He was friends with the in crowd and anyone who knew anyone. He also introduced me to my "play" cousin Ebie, whose father was the gangster rapper Eazy-E and her cousin Brittney. He brought me along to parties with Paris Hilton and her younger brother Barron, and had me party with Saudi royals, while we both put up a wall and a charade that we lived this awesome life and our parents were music industry power brokers.

Thanks to my mom's foresight, she pulled me out of public school and put me into a private one called Montclair Prep, where I would become friends with Tamara, whose dad eventually left her and her brother a construction empire. Tamara rubbed shoulders with the elite, including the Kardashians. Some of the wealthiest people's children also attended my school, especially if they found themselves with a record for being expelled from other exclusive programs, like me.

I had been kicked out of my middle school for flying into a rage and hurling profanities at the principal in the eighth grade. That behavior caused me not to be accepted at the private school I really wanted to go to: Campbell Hall.

Even still, I got a decent education and it helped me get into a university and brought me around people that most kids with my background would never have gotten the chance to. This afforded me the opportunity to meet and hang out with people who ingrained in me that I could make a difference in my life and in the lives of others as well. Although I ran with a good circle of people, I couldn't help feeling not truly accepted. Growing up, I was either too Black for the white kids, or I talked too "white" for the Black kids.

Going to Montclair didn't change that, it only made my differences glaringly obvious, or so I thought. While we had money like white people, it wasn't the same, and I would hear whispers that we were just "fronting," or living beyond our means. We obviously couldn't have been that wealthy—and no one else's parents knew mine.

"Their cars are leased," referring to the source of our wealth, some kid named Andrew gossiped after his upperclassmen friends revealed that my mom had learned about Montclair through another student when he came to Oracle to get rims for his Escalade. *Ha!*

"Yeah, right," I'd respond.

I would let it just roll off my back. I couldn't go around and blab about how I overheard my stepfather, Terry, tell my brother he forgot about $3,000,000, or that sometimes when I left school and went to the stash house, there would be millions of dollars on the floor. I would have to let them believe what they wanted.

Still, this didn't help my case with the other Black population at the school. Most of them were there on scholarships and they didn't accept me, either, because I wasn't one of them. Although my parents were from the hood, and made money in the hood from selling dope, I didn't come close to relating to them, or so they felt.

"He thinks he's all that." My good friend and classmate Justin relaid his thoughts of a new kid.

Life wouldn't just become easier or lose its hurdles after the petty dramas and simple worries of high school. As I transitioned into adulthood, I faced more insecurities and uncertainty about what or who I was. Now able to live without the burden of protecting my family secret, I still lived a life hampered by the weight of the family name. Growing up and experiencing being a part of something so captivating to the general public came with its own challenges and expectations.

Up until the day the indictment was revealed, I had no idea just how big and known my uncle Meech and the family had become to a wider audience. Soon after the raid, the arrest was broadcast throughout the country on separate TV and radio news stations. Announcing the end of one of the greatest distributions of cocaine runs in U.S. history—and the narcotics empire was pulled off by African Americans—was so blatant, it really affected me. Still, the kids at my school had no idea as they lived their own sheltered lives away from the media and the everyday problems of middle-class Americans. It wasn't just folklore, but a phenomenon never seen before, and it erupted and lay at the zeitgeist of hip-hop culture and mainstream media up until today.

Just like Trent, I didn't talk about it much or reveal who my parents were, but those around me would ask questions and make comments to others.

"What do his parents do?" a friend asked our close family associate Jermaine Dupri one late night at the club. The friend was a club promoter and came from a wealthy Lebanese family. He hadn't come across many young guys running in the same circles as me. He became curious to how and why I had come around.

Jermaine replied, "That's BMF. He Big Meech people."

After that, the greetings I would receive became warmer, and more invites would come in to exclusive parties in the hills and invite-only clubs from Hollywood to Malibu. I was a part of the in crowd—all because of my uncle and the effect he had on the industry. I didn't feel pride, but I didn't feel shame, either.

I had a certain amount of uneasiness that people looked to me to be some de-facto representative of my parents and the family; but no matter how hard I tried, or how quiet I was about my lineage, the word would get out and would spread. This would affect my development; it felt stifling but, in some circumstances, also empowering. I was able to go and experience things most could not—and all because of the name BMF. But in the same token, I was forbidden from being who I truly was or could develop into.

This attention would also bring unscrupulous characters and rumors that could tarnish not only the family name but myself and another son of a high-profile industry titan. Just before my eighteenth birthday, I would be introduced to Quincy, the son of Al B. Sure. My godsister, Bianca, was one of the first people to show him around Los Angeles after his mother, Kim, left Sean Combs for the final time. I would be brought into yet another circle of well-to-do children, but this time we would share similar backgrounds in ethnicity and the links between our parents.

Although I had never had the chance to know Quincy on a personal level, or anyone else through our shared connection, I was excited to build friendships with him and others in that circle. I believed that it would bring some familiarity to my life and I would be able to blend in, but again I felt like a sore thumb.

Slightly older and on my own, fighting the demons that came from my parents being away, I began drinking much sooner than Quincy and his circle of friends. I was determined not to be viewed in the same light as many of the individuals I recognized from my own personal experience: of only being around for the clout, the extravagant life, and the fame that came with being in that circle.

I relegated myself to the sidelines and made friends with the son of another West Coast producer and executive, who was known for his ruthless antics and unwavering rivalry with Puff, but still we became close, albeit a one-sided closeness, it seemed.

"So, do they not like you because you're . . ." I stopped short of the words that seemed most obvious to me.

Although everyone hung out, it seemed there was a brewing feud, or some people felt a way toward my new friend because he was gay, but that sexual preference, or how anyone else felt, did not bother me in the least.

"Of course not. We were together!" he claimed.

I wasn't sure if I believed him or not, but I thought his tales were amusing enough not only to listen to, but to make the naive mistake of telling my friend Justin. I believed he wouldn't share the information, especially since I was told it in confidence and wasn't sure if it was true. Justin would go on to share the information with his then-longtime girlfriend, who happened to also be sneaking around with a friend of Jessica's son, who went to the same public school.

In true fashion for gossip, by the time the story made its rounds and got back to me, it was I who had been with my so-called talkative friend. It was the furthest thing from the truth. Even still, it was a lesson that I actually didn't need to learn, coming from where I came from and grew up, but it caused me to question myself—not only as a friend, but as a man.

Those who once were my friends avoided me or spread more gossip. It was a female friend of mine, who at one point I had strong feelings for, who shared how those around me made fun of me and ridiculed my family. Apparently, when they desperately wanted cocaine for one of their nights out partying, one of these so-called friends would ponder aloud, "Maybe we can call Corey!"

It may have been hilarious to them, but it was a deep cut that I would harbor for a long time. I couldn't help who my parents were, or who I was, but others judged me. Ashamed, and rightfully so, I began to think it might actually be me; I considered how easy it was for people to turn their backs on others, how they could smile in my face and then make me the butt of their jokes when I wasn't within earshot. My curiosity piqued about being the subject of the conversation that put my own sexuality into question, and what that meant for me and for my family's image.

While my mom was away serving time, it was easy to put off the conversation and hide who I was, but all that would change once she returned home. Sooner or later, I would have to come clean, or be as honest as I could. Although it was my right, I felt that with my responsibility to the family, it would stand in the way of anything I wanted to accomplish.

Having my mother home, while I tried to find my place and co-exist with her, I began to think what I should do with my life. When we started our plans to tell my mother's story, the thoughts lingered in the back of my mind that those old skeletons could come back and derail everything we were working toward. People could use it to control me or discourage others from supporting us on our mission to change the narrative.

In 2015, I officially established and trademarked Black Mafia Family as a legitimate business. It was because of my desire to actually practice what I preached, and to live an authentic life, that I sought to start a business that was legitimate and would steer me away from my past of dealing marijuana—and that idea wouldn't come overnight.

Seeking inspiration, I didn't come up with the idea until watching *The Wolf of Wall Street,* more specifically the scene where Donnie Azoff, Jordan Belfort's business partner, while intoxicated from quaaludes, pulls out a shoe and brings up the brilliant idea that shoes could help their business's image. Similar to that concept, the bright idea that streetwear, with its almost synonymous connection to the streets where they earned their name—and the deeply entrenched styles of baseball caps and hoodies to the hood and drug dealers—would be a seamless transition away from what the family was known for to a symbol of what it represented in its positive light: family, unity, and ambition.

\* \* \*

Not soon afterward, and while wondering what exactly I was going to do, I was out at Club Greystone Manor. As I made my usual bar crawl, my old friend Albert from high school came from around the corner.

"Corey Mills, what's up, bro?" he greeted.

"What's up, bro? How have you been?" I replied back.

Albert's eyes lit up with excitement and he threw his hands up as if holding some invisible trophy. "Great, bro! Business took off!"

Albert, coincidentally enough, had started a hat business infusing exotic skins and leathers into team hats and was making nearly six figures each month. Just from the baseball cap side of it, the business was extraordinary, and I wanted a piece of it. Taking notes from a book I read, *Perfecting Your Pitch,* I readied a document to present to Albert proposing he make an exclusive collection of hats to send to certain celebrities to push our cause at Sylent Heart and to raise funds. Initially unmoved by my pitch, Albert resisted the idea, but we began to hang out and I would learn more about the business.

It wouldn't be until a chance encounter with another associate of his from Compton, with links to the rapper The Game, that he would become convinced. During the unofficial holiday of *420,* I dropped by Albert's place, where I would meet his friend Aaron, who chose not to smoke with me that night, for what I assumed was a territorial thing Blacks do around other Blacks when it comes to their white friends. However, it would be Albert who mentioned the name to Aaron and his attitude would change. Aaron had been the brain who told Albert to start Bompton, a small streetwear brand that Universal Music Group would later buy from him. Aaron became a trusted confidant, when it came to street culture, and Albert relied on him. In time, Aaron urged Albert to start a collaboration with me.

"Yo, bro! You gotta do a full collection!" Albert said excitedly at the other end of a phone call.

# THE WEIGHT OF RESPONSIBILITY

"I thought you weren't interested," I responded flatly.

"You explained it wrong!" he insisted.

Perhaps I had explained it wrong. It was hard to talk about something I lived and experienced firsthand rather than through the eyes of an onlooker. I had no idea the cultural impact my uncle Meech and stepfather, Terry, had on me up to that point. Of course, I explained it wrong; it was not only awkward to speak about my family, talking in what I felt was a boastful way, but to actually reveal who and what they were was an entirely new thing for me. How was I ever going to talk about my family in a way that didn't sound out of the norm to me, and didn't betray our code of honor? This marked the first time I was openly talking about it and facing the subject head-on.

For years, I kept my background a secret, but just like with my friends who truly knew me, it wouldn't be long before people wanted to know who my "people" were and what they did to make a living. I couldn't keep hiding from it, like I was ashamed, or it wasn't the elephant in the room. Somehow I had to find a way to embrace it without looking like a contradiction to the image I was now portraying with my mother and our foundation, and her getting her story out to the public. It would only be a matter of time before keeping it a secret wasn't an option anymore and it was best I take the reins on the narrative that was to be written.

*Why allow someone else to dictate our lives?*

In the beginning, I was laughed at and ridiculed, but the business started with a warm reception from its audience—and it only brought the spotlight on me closer. This applause would bring those in the family who disagreed with the idea to now vie for my spot or, at least, want the ownership of the trademark and the business. Talk about who I was, and how I became that, grew rampant and caused discord in my personal life.

Having already come out to my mom, my personal life felt like it was under a microscope. Soon I began to think even my own mother was against me. She hadn't really taken the news in the greatest way, but my delivery while out at a bar with my friends in a drunken stupor wasn't the proper forum, either. I often wondered how things would have turned out had she never left in the first place. I blamed her time away and the distance between us.

I knew I was harboring hatred deep inside me. Because of her chosen path, I didn't exactly feel free to be who I was or explore like other men at my age. Buried underneath responsibilities and expectations from the streets, I wasn't the best person to represent the family name.

Albeit more and more rappers and people around the world did embrace the brand and what it stood for, and soon studios would come calling. The naysayers who said that no studio would ever put up money on a production involving the BMF name or us were beginning to be silenced. Soon we would be summoned to meet with multiplatinum rapper 50 Cent. My mother and I scheduled a lunch meeting at the exclusive Soho House members club and met with him and Randall Emmett, his business partner at the time.

Insisting they weren't using the BMF name, but our participation was definitely wanted, my mother and I agreed to accept— only for petty rivalries to impede and we were ousted from the project. In turn, 50 Cent would go ahead and use the name BMF despite his repeated assertions that the project wouldn't use the moniker, which had been trademarked by me.

*What has happened to the family I knew?* I asked myself. No longer were we a united family, but it seemed prison and the time apart had made everyone strangers or, worse yet, rivals.

Out of greed, those who were once close to us were coming around again for what they could gain and would jump on the chance to take advantage of the mother-and-son–mending relationship to get what they wanted. The time apart had caused distrust, and although our love had been unwavering, we just absolutely didn't know each other as much as we thought we did. In hindsight, we both changed for what was the better, but in the present, it seemed like for the worse.

I have seen many of my goals realized and my mother's dreams coming true despite the many setbacks and disagreements. Although we have had mighty lows, we have endured and experienced immense highs, which made us triumphant and rise against the statistics that plague our communities. Prison and drugs shatter dreams and families, but through determination and resilience, many have defied the odds. Every day I work on myself to be a better son and to understand my mother, who is a human and a daughter, who grew up with her own insecurities and trauma, which have affected the way we communicate.

"I was a broke bitch, and so and so . . ." My mom began to vent one night, retelling the argument she had with my grandmother and how foul she had spoken to her. This came as a surprise because I had never heard my grandmother curse or put someone down, especially my mother.

However, it dawned on me in that moment: *That's the way you speak to me!*

I initially had no plans to let her decompress and tell me about the blowup they had, but this caught my attention. It felt like a message from God to be easy on my mother, as she, too, came from a dysfunctional household. Like me, she was only carrying the weight of her past and responsibility of her family before me. It made things easier to deal with and I was able to show more compassion, allowing for empathy in our own blowups. It gave me permission to forgive not only her, but others and myself as well.

Growing up with parents out in the streets, who are making an obscene amount of money, is not without its hardships. However, most of those difficulties are the results of our own reluctance to look within and find the patterns that we must utilize to break the generational curses that we place on ourselves out of ignorance. I was able to discover this through both my own self-journey and the shared journey with my mother, who is not only my rock, but a reflection of many of my own flaws.

# Chapter 23
# My Toni

*2017 to 2023*

Rᴇᴛᴜʀɴɪɴɢ ʜᴏᴍᴇ ꜰʀᴏᴍ ᴊᴀɪʟ ʙʀɪɴɢꜱ ɪᴛꜱ ᴏᴡɴ ᴛʀɪʙᴜʟᴀᴛɪᴏɴꜱ. Aꜱ ᴀ society, we don't sufficiently recognize the breakdown it creates in family bonds; people change after going away and suddenly they're like strangers to those with whom they live within close proximity. It's tough to adjust and I'm still a work in progress. But at least I'm still standing, still making it through what, for me, is now a totally different existence.

This moment brings me even deeper to the thought of the relationship I had with my mother. I often think about an argument we once had where I just wanted to set a boundary, no matter the differences or blowups we had between us. What I miss most are the calls I received from my mom every day; they weren't ever annoying or overbearing calls. Mom always had something interesting to talk about, even though people thought she was very serious. In fact, she was the total opposite, and I miss that about her. She kept me laughing. In retrospect, she was such a little lady with lots of spice. Just a year or two before her passing, we had the ugliest fight ever and didn't talk for months when finally my sister-in-law, at the time, called and said, "Come on, sis, you know Momma getting old. Call her!"

We apologized to each other and figured out how we both could've handled things better. However, we also agreed that sometimes arguments were necessary to see each other's point of view. Sometimes she forgot I didn't have it all figured out, like she was so used to. Things had changed in my time away, and not wanting to lead the same life meant making different decisions. No matter how hard or difficult the circumstances, and with the odds stacked against me, it wasn't ever easy to make the right choices, but I would learn to persevere with her support. I held in a lot, trying to keep a brave face, but I felt I was crumbling on the inside.

During our argument, her words hurt and had pushed me in a profound way to never let anything or anyone deter me, even if it meant becoming someone I had never been. It prodded me to believe in things that I had never thought possible. It's our talks that held me together, especially after the reconciliation that still brings me peace today.

The day we reconciled, we talked all day long. Two days later, I was flying back to Detroit to hang out with my best friend, my mom. I don't know what got into Mom, but I felt like she was different, acting so spontaneously and adventurous. I would laugh and think, *Who is this lady who says she wants to go dancing and hang out with me and my friends?* After having a girls' day out with all my friends and family, and taking in a screening of *Girls Trip,* my girlfriends would urge her on while they recorded her dancing and singing along to Future's "Wicked."

"A wiggle, a wiggle . . . wiggle . . . wiggle!" she sang as she wiggled her little five-foot-one frame in a video shared on Instagram.

Like two peas in a pod, we shared so many similarities. Dealing with infidelity while standing by our husbands, and simultaneously providing for our family, she was the lady I always wanted to be. Even sharing the same interest in thrillers and sappy romcoms, we shared this love as we flicked through the television, always looking for something good to watch. We were up late one night watching Lifetime movies together when a commercial aired about a cruise vacation. She abruptly turned to me and said, "Toni, let's go on a cruise."

"Okay!" I replied enthusiastically.

"This week!" she said pointedly.

I thought for sure she meant sometime in the near future, but no, we immediately got on the computer and booked a five-day/four-night cruise through the Caribbean that summer and followed it with traveling throughout the States, hitting Miami, Louisiana for Essence Fest, and Vegas. Just as we got back, she was already planning our next trip, but then I got a call to do an event in LA. I needed to be there the following Monday.

My mom's look of disappointment brought a bit of uncertainty for me as I wondered why she was suddenly so eager to go on many trips, when she had never been prompted to travel this often. The thought of missing a rare opportunity that could help me financially felt too hard to refuse, so I said yes to the impromptu business trip. I accepted the offer and told my mother it would be a short trip and I would be back the following week.

"I need to go make this money," I tried to explain to her.

"You don't need money as long as I got it," she said reassuringly while holding her arms open for an embrace as I was leaving and heading to the airport.

"That's your money, Mom. I've been here all summer, and I need to make my own money." I was too independent for my mom to take care of me. I always wanted to take care of her. "I'll be back the following Sunday," I reassured her.

Just before I left that Sunday, Mom came begging me to take a picture. I really didn't want to take it, because my hair wasn't done, and I wasn't properly dressed.

"Come on, Toni, you look fine," she egged me on.

She kept urging me until I caved in and, after getting as presentable as I possibly could, posed for a selfie with my niece, granddaughter, her, and myself in the center. You never know why things happen, but it would be one of the last and only pictures of four generations of us ladies in the family. It's something I can never replicate and a time that'll only live on in my memory to cherish for the rest of my life.

As I arrived in LA ready for business, I headed to the bank where my banker had instructed me to go. "Ms. Welch, where have you been? I haven't seen you all summer. "How was your summer?" he asked.

"I had the best summer ever!" I responded cheerfully.

It wasn't a lie; I literally did have an unforgettable summer. I shared with him about my recent travels and how great it was getting to experience new places with my mom. I stressed how much we don't appreciate getting that time with our parents as we become adults and have our own children, but it was something I felt we both needed, especially after being away for so long. There was no denying that I wanted to spend as much time as I could with my mom. I dreaded having to inform her I would once again be leaving to go on more business trips, since she had made more plans for another vacation.

Not ever thinking it would be the last time I would get to see my little lady, I could hardly contain my excitement in knowing that I was going right back to her. It would be just the two of us: me and my best friend; "my Toni," as she used to call me. During the end of our voyage on the cruise, my mom made plans and demanded we dress up in the same color scheme so that we could take the best Mother-Daughter photo at the dress-up dinner.

Unfortunately, we were never able to see or receive the pictures, as we returned late back to the boat the last night after our excursions on land. The boat crew had already destroyed the pictures. Despite her demands to speak to the captain or anyone in charge, we weren't able to view or get them. They were gone forever and all we had were the memories we made together. She was livid; although we had plenty of pictures from our phones, they couldn't replace the professional ones taken while in the dining room of the ship, or just the absolute bliss we felt in that moment. As I reflect back, everything seemed to mean more, and every moment started to count.

This experience made me think about each death of the people closest to me. When my brother died, that was my first painful hurt after not speaking for quite a while. I loved my brother deeply, he almost couldn't do any wrongs in my eyes—even with his and Terry's big fallout, in which Terry accused him of stealing his watch and banned him from coming around. My brother had moved to Florida, and I hadn't talked to him, even though I didn't believe he was the thief.

After months without hearing from him, he called before his death and said, "Hi, sis. I love you and I miss you. I'll be coming back to Detroit this week and I want to see you."

I was so happy to hear his voice, and I planned my flight to meet him there, but before I could get there, he was gone. Now I see why those pictures were so important and why that summer was the best one I'd ever had. It was just my mom and me. God knew I was going to need that memory.

A few months later, in October of 2019, my mother called me on a Wednesday night saying she couldn't breathe. I felt like I couldn't breathe as a feeling of hopelessness instantly warped my brain from making any decisions. I moved around frantically, jumping from the bed and pulling out a duffel bag, throwing anything wearable into the small travel bag.

"Just go!" Corey said calmly, giving me a sense of reassurance that things would be okay, but I was too far away.

The situation ended up being hopeless. It was late Wednesday, early Thursday morning that I had gotten Mom's distress call, and by Friday my world had once again been turned upside down. My first love was gone.

"I hate October!" I exclaimed to my friend Dr. Toby. We sat in his office one afternoon discussing where my life was in that moment and how I was feeling. After my mother's death, October was the month I dreaded the most. Nothing good seemed to ever come of it.

"Why do you dread that particular month so much, Tonesa?" Dr. Toby wanted to know.

"Well, where do I start? My brother was killed on Halloween. I got really ill in October. I was indicted in October, went to prison in the same month, and it's also the month that my mother died." Exasperated just from saying it all out loud, I slumped farther down in the chair sitting opposite him.

"Have you ever thought about changing your perspective?" he asked.

I stared blankly at him. How could I change my perspective on so many negative events that happened in my life, all in the same cold and dreary month, at the beginning of fall? He chuckled and gestured with his hands to slow down.

"I know, I know. It seems odd to hear, for some of those situations aren't easy to get over, if ever, but have you ever thought that instead of dreading and putting so much bad energy toward what could come in October, try to think of what blessings may happen during that time?"

He was right. I had never thought about that. I would just repeatedly tell anyone I encountered how bad a month it was, as if almost predicting the outcome before it could even arrive. That maybe in some way I manifested those things in my life around that time because the cold brought so many painful memories rather than joy, like most would expect with the coming holidays.

I only felt forbearance as the seasons changed and couldn't see the possibilities that my new life could bring.

"How about thinking of the great blessings that come in the fall? The chance for reflection and change, instead of death and turmoil?" His question echoed through my innermost being. The thought that death wasn't to mourn, but to celebrate life and reflect on how to honor those I had lost and the life I once had lived. It would mean living to my fullest potential and putting away the hurt and regret that I had held on to for so long. With it came the possibility of embracing all those changes that had once left me defeated, and they now could be harnessed and used as armor. I could honor my strength to keep going, not only for myself but my family.

In the time since then, October has started to change for me. I've been brought truly amazing opportunities that I would otherwise not have capitalized on, had I stayed stuck in the defeatist mindset. I had to embrace October, like it was a time of celebration and an opportunity on how far I had come from being just a little Black girl from a little street named Coyle, to a woman changing the narrative and righting the wrongs of her past.

After being snubbed from the production of the series, I was able to sign my own deal telling just my story through my lens and the truth about who I was. Fittingly, it premiered on BET+ in the month of October, and I hosted events for Vice President Kamala Harris, and received many other blessings, and I'm sure more will come in the same month I once dreaded.

Dr. Toby completely transformed my thinking. It was no longer about just letting go of the past, taking accountability, and forgiving myself, but finding an entirely new way of life. How could I expect and find more prosperity if I didn't do the very thing that mattered most, which was examining and coming up with an entirely new way of thinking? While in prison in the drug program, one of the courses taught was criminal thinking. It was a close examination of who we were, to the utmost core of our being. I, like every other woman there, had a real issue with the way I saw things, and I quite routinely solved issues in a criminal matter. No time for due process, or waiting for the best way to handle it, or letting God handle it. I was busy trying to handle things in my own way and time and was always coming up short. This affected my prospects before they could even become prospects. Just like the talk I posted on my Instagram reflecting on who I was had brought me opportunities, which I would never have had—if I allowed myself to operate the way I once was.

This was inherently embedded in me from a young age. Yes, it wasn't entirely my fault how I came up, but it was entirely up to me to change the narrative. Just as much as I realized that I was blessed to get such a short sentence, I was just as blessed to have been sent to prison. Growing up with all brothers, I spent so much time trying to keep up and show I was just as strong as Ernest and Darry that I did anything to prove it. I was willing to scrape up my knees and get cuts and bruises from hopping gates, climbing trees, and fixing up cars. In the same manner, I wanted to keep up with them in the streets. I wouldn't let anyone outhustle me or any of the men I was with. This route would have led to only two things: an even more lengthy prison sentence or death. I would have drunk and drugged myself straight off the top of Mulholland Drive, had the Feds not come and intervened in the time that they did. It wasn't easy to accept that, but in the time of being released, I knew it wouldn't have been any other way.

Shit, any longer in the streets and my two other boys would probably have followed in my footsteps, as their oldest brother did, and they would've ended up with painfully long prison sentences. In my eyes, none of them were built for that street life and were not supposed to spend the majority of their adult lives in prison. I had done that and took those risks to provide an even better life for them, even though it ended up that they'd have a less opulent life than I had.

# MY TONI

The ramifications of my life hit them hard. I was unable to protect my eldest from his own decisions and he, too, ended up incarcerated, causing a cycle with his own daughter, just like my own children, where he was away for most of her adolescent life. He did much of his growing up in prison, while the other two suffered and thrived in varying degrees before they, too, would show signs of the effects this life had on those left behind.

Dealing with his own sexuality and insecurities, Corey would suffer drug addictions and brief homelessness, while Jason went on to get married and have three beautiful daughters. I think the weight of the unknown and abrupt lifestyle change was heavy on Jason's heart.

In June 2023, my middle son would shatter my heart when I received a call that he had taken his own life. I can't begin to describe the empty hole left in Jason's wake or how to tell anyone that no parent should ever have to bury their own child. Just like my mother had told me, it was an indescribable pain. When loved ones pass from old age or sickness, or even some unfortunate violence, it comes with an utterly different form of unpacking than when it comes to suicide.

I still wrestle with, *Is there more that I could have done? If I had never chosen this life or ever moved to California, would things have been different?* You can't hide from the guilt or the agony of not being able to save or just be there for one of your babies.

Having to face my granddaughters, and not finding the words to explain why they will never see their father again, is one of the hardest things I've ever had to do. It's hard not to blame certain decisions, actions, or who plays a part in that situation, but reaching back to the teachings of Dr. Toby, I knew to find some peace in living for my son in a way that would make him proud and my granddaughters as well.

# Epilogue

"SHE WAS RIGHT ABOUT EVERYTHING," HAROLD SAID FLATLY while we were having dinner with Corey. After going through so much together, no matter how ugly the past, we still share a son and try our best to be there for him. "Yeah, she said she brought the drugs to me, but that's not true. I introduced it to her, and she turned around and brought back better."

Corey and I chuckled as Harold gave out a hearty laugh, retelling the story.

"I'm sorry. I was young and I just didn't know," I admitted.

Harold struggled to find the right words in that moment, but I now understand how much this simple gesture meant. It wasn't simply for one situation, but many, and not so much what he had done to me, but for the times he hadn't listened when his best interest was in mind.

Honestly, how can I stay mad when for the most part of my life, I didn't listen to the best advice or believe in myself the way I did the men in my life. Sure, the lack of my biological father's presence, my constant need for reassurance from my brothers and stepfather, all played a part in me carrying those issues over to my relationships and having doubt in myself. It was still no coincidence that many things I said or had done helped them get to where they were; yet it would take me well into my fifties to discover that the only one I truly needed was myself.

It doesn't seem like a factor, but the fear of returning to prison is in every person who has served time. When I was released from prison, 38 percent of the women released that year would return to prison within five years. The first five years of my release were more difficult than the time served in prison. I was faced with financial difficulties, family dynamics that had shifted and changed, for the most part in a downward spiral; and without rules and regulations, I was now matched with wrestling the past me and the new me I wanted to be.

Unable to pay small bills and struggling to make the rent, and halfway never making ends meet, was a stress and a challenge I hadn't faced in so long, if ever. Still, I was able to do it by believing in my support system and finally listening to the little Black girl inside. If I could be a part of and help build a drug empire, then I certainty could find a way to reinvent myself and become a productive member of society.

Even with the doubters who didn't believe that I, or anyone else like me, can change, and the other well-meaning family and friends who attempted to convince me to get back involved in the drug trade, I remembered those criminal-thinking courses and the struggle it had been to get through prison. Just as much as Robin and I had done before in the past through ignorance, without a doubt, I know in my heart I have more purpose and drive to continue and do something that will have a lasting impact.

"They always gone be like that," my mother, Carol, said one day after I returned home, defeated. One of the cast members of my first television series had just sent a scathing email to the network brass demanding they take the show down and disparaging my character.

**Tonesa is a drug dealer. I don't respect or associate with her type,** the email began.

She threatened legal action against the production company

and network for simply not focusing on her so-called brand in the way they did the other ladies of the show, or so she claimed. She had hardly put together a business and had thrown some impromptu get-togethers to showcase the lackluster beauty products she had begun to make. When the editor on the show failed to extend or make magic happen—where there was none—she quickly blamed me and used my past and attacked me. This threatened the longevity of the show, which was initially a success, and was hopeful for a renewal, but it was squandered away after she didn't get her way.

How could she or anyone else not see how this affected me? It hurt that someone I thought I could trust would betray me in such a manner that it would affect my income and new life, but remembering my mother's wise words gave me strength that no matter what, there will be haters, and those who don't care to see you win or who will count you out. They used every bit of me, at every turn they could, and when things seemed hopeless, they easily threw me away.

I'm no longer who I thought I was. I think in a way I'm apt to find love and see love—and not in the form of another person—but inside I have this compassion and see people differently. My love is for myself, and every day, no matter the circumstances, I can say, "I'll be okay." Understanding that I'll be okay has helped me show trust in others and find comfort that my sons will also be all right.

Coming home from prison, I appeared to come off overbearing, especially for Corey. I wanted to know where he was going, who he would be with, and when he would return. I don't know why, but I just had this foreboding feeling that something terrible would happen to him. I think any mother worries about their sons, especially when they make lifestyle choices that so many others don't agree with. It made me worry in an unrealistic way.

Perhaps I could have helped Jason more, had I thought he needed it, but he was the independent one who stayed in his room or wanted to do his own thing and found comfort in the hood with his boys. With a full beard at thirteen, he appeared more of an adult than he was. I didn't think my absence could have done so much to him, or any of the rest of my family.

During this time, Corey seemed to adapt like a chameleon, similar to both his father and me. Marlon flourished even under such circumstances, and my other relatives either stood by my side or saw it as a chance to attack and take what they could. I, however, have overcome every moment I felt defeated or afraid of.

I'm strong.

Getting closer to God and finding my understanding happened one day during Bible study when I shared this dream: I was sitting at a big table with my brothers sharing a meal when suddenly things began to be taken from me. First I noticed the turkey had disappeared from the table, and I remarked how I didn't have a home anymore; then more and more platters filled with jewelry and other things were disappearing as well.

My Bible study teacher said, "I want you to read Job. It is not the subject we are covering today, but you are describing the story of Job in the Bible. I feel you're a modern-day female version of Job and that's why God put you in the desert."

Right then and there, I realized the path I had taken in my life started with me when I was a little girl. I always felt different, and I never understood this feeling. I never felt like anyone else. Ending up in prison in the pit, hiding in the closet when I was little, and all of that, seemed to stem from my faith in God. As I read a mantra from Wayne Dyer, I began to recite it every day as I began to find my faith in God. In the end, the things and people around us didn't matter. Even as a kid, I hid behind the clothes and every other little thing that money could buy. I hid behind material things and what I could do for people to hide away from my insecurities.

If there was any doubt left, it was stripped away from my middle son's death—the last bit of it I had for myself. I gained a profound understanding of who I was, and today I can feel confident in the skin God gave me. I can feel proud of me. I have overcome so many things I never could imagine.

Now I am more than just that little Black girl or some drug queen, but a woman who knows her own worth. No longer am I putting too much attention on a man's word and his actions. I can decipher what's worth my time and what isn't. Not only am I avoiding the fast-money options with the heavy penalties if caught, but I am entirely disinterested in associating with or being around those who still want to be a part of the system that destroys the very neighborhoods I grew up in.

I find myself around other strong and powerful women who are making a difference in the world and effecting change. Once too shy or worried that these ladies wouldn't want to be my friend, I find myself with a seat at the table. Most of my life, I avoided policymakers and politicians; now I partake in writing motions and speaking with those on both sides of the aisle to fight for those who still don't have a voice.

Having found my inner strength, I've discovered it's not always about the man. Sure, I can still tap into the confidence I had making those moves on the street, but a different mindset now helps me capitalize on the opportunities that keep coming my way. Knowing I can make it on my own is so empowering—as is building a whole different legacy that my granddaughters will be proud of.

# Acknowledgments

First and foremost, I would like to extend my deepest gratitude to my son Corey, whose unwavering support and creative spirit have been the heartbeat of this book. Corey, your insightful words and unique biography not only added depth to our narrative, but also illuminated our journey with your wisdom. Your ability to see the world with such a fresh perspective has been both inspiring and grounding. Thank you for your patience, encouragement, and for always believing in the power of my story.

Collaborating with you on this first book has been a dream come true. I am immensely proud of what we have achieved together, and more so, I am proud of the wonderful person you are. With all my love and appreciation, your mom.

To my brothers, Ernest Welch and Kevin Thomas, and my sister, Joyce Banks: thank you for being my support and for always being there for me. I'm so grateful for the love and the special bond we share.

I also would like to extend my deepest gratitude to our incredible editor, Leticia Gomez. Your keen eye for detail, unwavering patience, and insightful guidance have polished this work to perfection. Without your dedication and expertise, this book would not be what it is today. Your belief in my vision and ability to transform words into something truly meaningful is both humbling and inspiring.

I also wish to express my sincere thanks to my literary agent, Frank Weimann. Your enthusiasm and tireless advocacy for our book have made this journey possible. Thank you for navigating the complexities of the publishing world with skill and grace, and for being a steadfast supporter from day one. Your strategic

# ACKNOWLEDGMENTS

prowess and unwavering faith in Corey's work have not only opened doors, but have also opened minds. Together, both of you have made this book a reality, and for that, we're genuinely grateful. Thank you for believing in this story and for the countless hours you dedicated to realizing it.